IN OLD PHOTO

C000283856

AROUND HAYES
& WEST DRAYTON
TRANSPORT & INDUSTRY

PHILIP SHERWOOD

SUTTON PUBLISHING

Sutton Publishing Limited
Phoenix Mill · Thrupp · Stroud
Gloucestershire · GL5 2BU

First published 2004

Title page photograph: A protest meeting in
Harmondsworth, 7 June 2003.

British Library Cataloguing in Publication Data
A catalogue record for this book is available from the
British Library.

ISBN 0-7509-3669-X

Typeset in 10.5/13.5 Photina.
Typesetting and origination by
Sutton Publishing Limited.
Printed and bound in England by
J.H. Haynes & Co. Ltd, Sparkford.

Philip Sherwood is a retired chemist turned local historian who as a
Principal Scientific Officer in the Scientific Civil Service has worked for the
Transport (formerly Road) Research Laboratory and for the Royal
Commission on Environmental Pollution. He is an active member of several
amenity and environmental groups, the Publications Editor of the Hayes and
Harlington Local History Society and former Chairman of the local branch
of the Campaign for the Protection of Rural England. He has compiled three
previous publications in this series: *Around Hayes & West Drayton In Old
Photographs* (1996), *Around Hayes & West Drayton: A Second Selection* (1998)
and *Around Hayes & West Drayton: A Third Selection* (2002). In a related
series, he is also author of *Heathrow: 2000 Years of History* (1999).

CONTENTS

An 1880s Ordnance Survey map of the area between West Drayton and Botwell (Hayes). This is almost in the centre of the area covered by this book and shows how the canal (1794) and railway line (1838) run almost parallel to each other. At this time brick-making was the major manufacturing industry, centred on the small hamlet of Starveall (later renamed Stockley). Several brickfields developed in the area close to the canal, which enabled cheap and effective transport of the bricks to the London market. Within the next twenty-five years the Hayes Development Company would introduce many more industries to the triangular area, marked A on the map, bordered by Dawley Road, the canal and the railway line. This led to the rapid industrialisation of Hayes, which developed within three decades from a rural village to an industrial town.

ACKNOWLEDGEMENTS

Sincere thanks are due to all the many people who have helped in providing information and photographs for inclusion in this book. These include Carolynne Cotton and Gwyn Jones of the Hillingdon Local Studies, Archives and Museum Service in Uxbridge Library; Ray Smith of the West Drayton and District Local History Society; Terry White of the Hayes and Harlington Local History Society; Audrey Beasley, Josh Hayles, John Laker, Dave McCartney, John McDonnell, Rose McManus, the late Josh Marshall, Ken Pearce, Douglas Rust, James Skinner, Pete Sluman, Graham Smeed and John Walters. The individuals and the commercial organisations that provided illustrative material are acknowledged, where appropriate, in the captions to the relevant photographs. Where no source is given the illustration is taken from the author's collection. The following abbreviations are used in the credits: HHLHS – the Hayes and Harlington Local History Society; WDLHS – the West Drayton and District Local History Society.

INTRODUCTION

According to Francis Bacon (1561–1626), there are three things that make a nation great and prosperous – 'a fertile soil, busy workshops, and easy conveyance for men and commodities from one place to another'. West Middlesex at one time had all three in abundance but developments and 'improvements' in the 'easy conveyance' of 'men and commodities' has meant that the fertile soil and busy workshops have been destroyed or taken over by the growth in transport and communications.

Until well into the twentieth century such growth and improvement was considered to be synonymous with progress but it is becoming increasingly apparent that the disadvantages of improving the transport infrastructure may well outweigh the advantages. Transport provides a clear example of how some choices exclude others and bring about a situation that far from being better is actually worse. Cars and aeroplanes have brought a freedom to travel that hitherto was enjoyed only by the very rich. But as more and more people exercise that freedom it has brought congestion and pollution, made streets into places that are no longer safe for children, and has even threatened the rights of people to live at peace within their own homes. A series of decisions that appeared to be perfectly justifiable at the time they were made has led to an outcome that no rational person would have wished for.

The good communications of west Middlesex arise from its position on flat ground to the west of London. Consequently travellers between London and the West Country and south Midlands have always had to pass through it, and with the advent of aviation the existence of a flat landscape with good rail and road links made the area a natural choice for the capital's major airport. The area is traversed by three historic routes: the Exeter road (A30), which follows an earlier Roman route, and the post-Roman Bath (A4) and Oxford (A40) roads. These were turnpiked in the early eighteenth century and all three became important stagecoach routes. Several relics of the stagecoach era remain, particularly in Colnbrook, the first major stopping point on the journey from London to Bath.

The area was opened up to its first industrial development by the Grand Junction (now Grand Union) Canal, which links the Midlands with the Thames at Brentford. It was opened in 1794, and although it had little effect on the traffic using the roads, it encouraged industry, notably brick-making. In 1838 the Great Western Railway line was opened through the area, and between Hayes and West Drayton the railway and the canal run almost side by side, both affording good communications with London. Many factories established themselves in the area between the railway line and the canal, and Hayes became an increasingly important industrial town.

The opening of the railway dramatically reduced traffic on the main roads, which fell to 25 per cent of its previous intensity, and for the next sixty years the roads were a minor source of transport. With the advent of motorised traffic in the early 1900s, the importance of the road network was renewed, and by the 1920s road traffic had increased to such a degree that new bypass roads had to be opened to take traffic away from the A4, A30 and A40 and relieve bottlenecks at towns such as Brentford, Hounslow, Uxbridge and Colnbrook. But even these bypass roads became inadequate as road traffic continued to increase, a situation exacerbated by the opening of factories and ribbon development along these roads. The A30, A4 and A40 were therefore bypassed in their turn by the M3, M4 and M40 and these were later linked together by the M25.

Last, but by no means least, the development of Heathrow airport since 1944 has transformed the area, much of which has been completely engulfed by the airport and its approach roads, and now even more of the area is threatened by current proposals to expand the airport to the north of the A4.

The development of transport in the area is a good example of Sewill's law which claims that a new form of mass transport emerges about every fifty years, i.e. 1750 – canals; 1800 – turnpike roads and stagecoaches; 1850 – railways; 1900 – the motor car; 1950 – civil aviation.

The inexorable growth of the transport infrastructure has eventually come to threaten any development other than that associated with transport. First came the virtual destruction of the once prosperous agricultural industry. This was followed by the flight of various manufacturing industries as they found it more economic to move to locations where land and labour were cheaper, to other parts of the country initially, and latterly to the Far East. What was once a diverse economy based on the manufacture of a wide range of products has become an economy increasingly dependent on aviation-based service industries arising from Heathrow Airport's inexorable expansion. As industries have closed down factories many of the sites have been taken over by organisations associated with Heathrow, which are not labour-intensive: in many instances the sites of former factories are occupied by warehouses where the number of people employed is minimal.

This book describes the history of water, road, rail and air transport in the area around Hayes and West Drayton, and then goes on to consider how development of the transport infrastructure has contributed first to the growth and then to the decline of local industry. Finally it looks into the future to consider whether it is possible for the transport infrastructure to continue to grow without there being appalling environmental consequences.

P.T. Sherwood
Harlington 2004

1

Road Transport

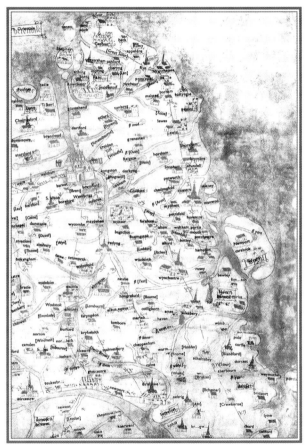

Gough's map of southern England. This, the earliest known map of the British Isles, dates from about 1360; the cartographer is unknown but it is known as Gough's map after the name of the publisher in the eighteenth century. The southern portion of this map, shown above, is peculiar because east is at the top and by modern standards the rivers are given prominence out of all proportion to their size. Roads are marked but only very faintly and through West Middlesex the roads that would become the modern A4, A30 and A40 are shown as are Uxbridge (Waxsbrigg) and Colnbrook (Colbrok).

Inland carriage of goods and people has always existed. However, until the eighteenth century, apart from the brief spell of Roman occupation, roads were so bad that wheeled transport could not be used for much of the year. Goods were therefore carried as far as possible by river with only the final part of the journey being undertaken across land. To the south the Thames was (and still is) navigable as far as Oxford, to the west the Colne was navigable as far as Uxbridge and in the east the Lea was navigable as far as Hertford. *(Uxbridge Library)*

The western portion of John Norden's map of Middlesex. Even 200 years after Gough's map the first reasonably accurate map of Middlesex, drawn by John Norden in about 1590 and published in 1610, still gave prominence to the rivers without any mention of roads. Norden's map is of interest because all the local towns and villages are marked and most of them appear on a map for the very first time. No roads are shown but the map reveals that there was a bridge at Cranford.

A packhorse train (from Hadfield's *British Canals*). Whenever possible goods were carried by boats on the rivers to the nearest point to their destination, but the final part of the journey still had to be made by road. The local road network started as foot and horse-drawn traffic along tracks that developed into roads linking the villages in the area. Although the dictionary definition of a road is 'a track suitable for wheeled traffic', implying the existence of some sort of weather-proof surface, this was far from the case, and during wet weather 'roads', little more than trackways, became impassable to wheeled traffic. For this reason much was carried on the backs of horses and mules.

The deplorable condition of the road network existed from the earliest times up to the end of the seventeenth century, except for the 400-year period of Roman occupation. The Romans built a network of properly engineered roads that connected the major towns of Roman Britain. In West Middlesex the only major Roman road ran from London to Bath via Silchester (the route of the modern A30); neither the Bath road (A4) nor the Oxford road (A40) is of Roman origin.

However, apart from major roads Britain had an extensive network of other Roman roads that connected smaller towns and villages. One such is believed to have run from Verulamium (St Albans) to the south coast via Uxbridge and Staines. Hatch Lane, Harmondsworth, is thought to be part of this route and before it was obliterated by Heathrow airport there was a continuation of this lane for about a half-mile south of the Bath Road known as Long Lane. Hatch Lane and Long Lane between them were a mile long and are remarkably straight, but the extent to which this was a proper road in the modern sense rather than a well-defined track is unknown.

The Roman roads were built primarily for military purposes so that the Legions could move quickly to any potential trouble spots. However, they were, of course, also used for the passage of goods and people and were so well built that they continued to be used long after the Romans had left. For example, in the autumn of 1066, when England was expecting an invasion from Normandy, news came of an invasion from Norway on the coast of Yorkshire. King Harold promptly marched his army to Stamford Bridge near York where he overwhelmingly defeated the Norwegians on 25 September. Four days later he was told that the Normans had landed in Sussex and the English army marched the 250 miles from Stamford Bridge to Hastings in nine days, only to be defeated on 14 October. An army could only have made the journey to Yorkshire and back in such a short time if the roads it travelled on were in good condition. King Harold and his men were, of course, exhausted by the time they got back and it is arguable that had the roads been worse and they had taken longer the outcome of the battle would have been quite different.

With the departure of the Romans in the early fifth century the road network such as it was fell into chaos. Apart from the few major Roman roads that remained other parts of the network were nothing more than tracks often completely impassable to wheeled vehicles in wet weather. Until the sixteenth century the manors and their inhabitants were generally liable for the upkeep of the roads but the extent to which this was done depended on the whims of those nominally responsible – there was no central authority to ensure that they fulfilled any obligations that they might have. Road maintenance therefore meant little more than the removal of impediments to the traveller in order to maintain a right of passage.

In 1555 an Act of Parliament was passed giving individual parishes throughout the country the statutory responsibility for the upkeep of the roads within their boundaries. Every parish thus became the local highway authority and every able-bodied man was required to perform six days of unpaid labour a year in helping with the maintenance of the road. Not surprisingly road administration under the 1555 Act was never very effective as the workers lacked the skills, finance and enthusiasm to do a good job. This was particularly the case (as in many of the local villages) where the village centre was well away from the main road which meant that the main beneficiaries were travellers from distant towns rather than the local inhabitants. The parishioners were likely to concentrate their road mending-activities on the roads which they themselves were likely to use and as a result the trunk roads were very poorly maintained.

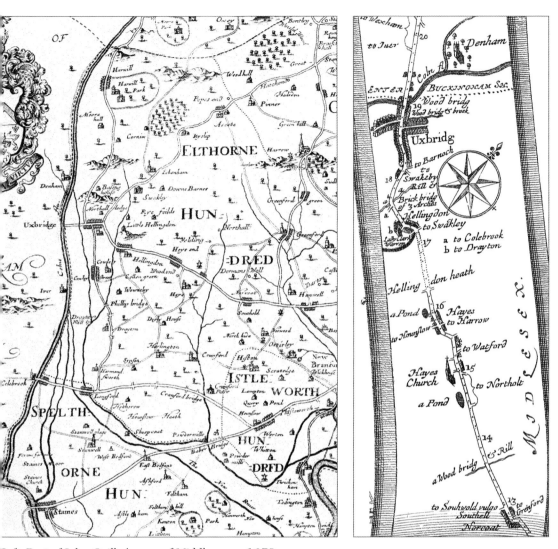

Left: Part of John Ogilby's map of Middlesex, *c.* 1670.

Right: A section of Ogilby's map of the Uxbridge Road from Southall to Uxbridge, *c.* 1675. In 1654 provision was made for a highway rate to be paid in place of statute labour but it was becoming apparent that the system was failing to provide the roads that changing economic circumstances demanded. Roads were becoming an increasingly important means of communication, and this is reflected in the maps of the late seventeenth century where they are depicted in some detail for the first time. For example, Ogilby's map of Middlesex not only depicts the main roads through the area but also most of the minor roads connecting the local towns and villages, he went even further and also published a series of road maps for travellers (above right). *(Uxbridge Library)*

A N

A   C   T

O F

P A R L I A M E N T

To continue and render more effectual three Acts for repairing the Highways between Tyburn *and* Uxbridge, *in the County of* Middlesex; *and for amending the Road leading from* Brent Bridge *over* Hanwell Heath, *through the Parishes of* Hanwell, New Brentford, *and* Ealing, *to the Great Western Road in the said County; and for lighting, watching, and watering the High-way between* Tyburn *and* Kensington Gravel Pits.

O X F O R D:

PRINTED AT THE CLARENDON PRESS.

M. DCC. LXIX.

The amended Turnpike Act for the Uxbridge road, 1769. An Act of Parliament was passed in 1714 that empowered trustees to collect tolls for repairing and amending the highways between Tyburn and Uxbridge. Several later acts were passed that altered and enlarged the powers of the original act. (*Uxbridge Library*)

With the beginning of the Industrial Revolution in the early eighteenth century, however, there was a rapid expansion in the amount of traffic using the roads. Together with the poor maintenance of the road network this caused serious problems and prompted the government to take action. Being reluctant to finance the maintenance of the roads the government fell back on a solution very similar to present-day Private Finance Initiatives. Private companies called Turnpike Trusts were established, the first one being created in 1706. The public was given the opportunity to invest in these companies, and the money raised by the trusts was split between profits for the shareholders and the cost of maintaining the roads in the control of the trust. Travellers paid to use the roads, and toll-gates (also known as turnpikes from the spikes placed on top of the gates to prevent people from jumping over) were established at which people and carriages had to pay a toll before they could pass and continue with their journey. Following the passing of the Turnpike Act in 1706 it was not long before both the Uxbridge and the Bath roads were turnpiked.

Within the area of the Uxbridge road covered by this book the Tyburn to Uxbridge Turnpike Trust erected two toll-gates – one at Hayes Bridge *(above)* and one near the Greenway in Uxbridge *(below)*. The toll-gate at Hayes Bridge (Hayes Gate) is viewed looking towards Southall and dates from the early nineteenth century. The picture of the Hillingdon Turnpike dates from about 1840 and shows the view looking towards Uxbridge. The buildings in the left background of this picture are still identifiable; the present-day Turnpike Lane is on the extreme left and RAF Uxbridge is on the right. *(Above: HHLHS; Below: Uxbridge Library)*

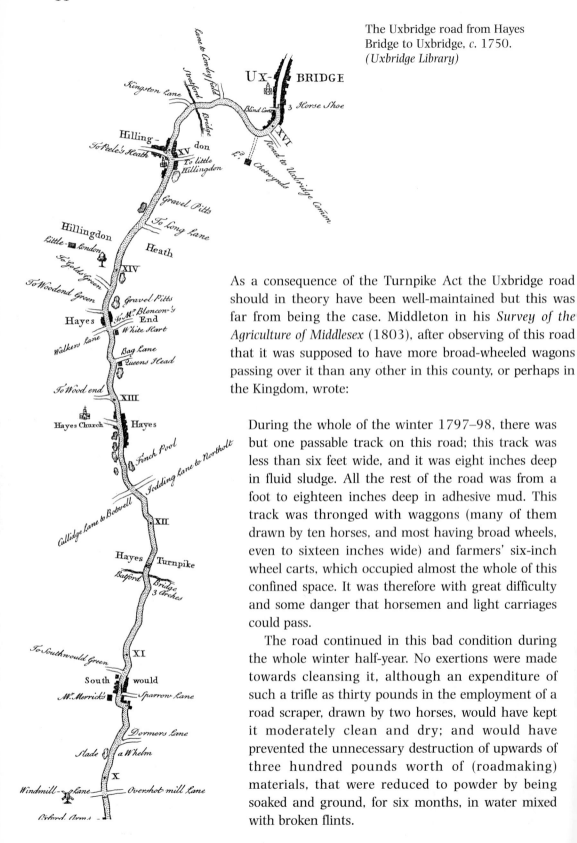

The Uxbridge road from Hayes Bridge to Uxbridge, *c.* 1750. (*Uxbridge Library*)

As a consequence of the Turnpike Act the Uxbridge road should in theory have been well-maintained but this was far from being the case. Middleton in his *Survey of the Agriculture of Middlesex* (1803), after observing of this road that it was supposed to have more broad-wheeled wagons passing over it than any other in this county, or perhaps in the Kingdom, wrote:

During the whole of the winter 1797–98, there was but one passable track on this road; this track was less than six feet wide, and it was eight inches deep in fluid sludge. All the rest of the road was from a foot to eighteen inches deep in adhesive mud. This track was thronged with waggons (many of them drawn by ten horses, and most having broad wheels, even to sixteen inches wide) and farmers' six-inch wheel carts, which occupied almost the whole of this confined space. It was therefore with great difficulty and some danger that horsemen and light carriages could pass.

The road continued in this bad condition during the whole winter half-year. No exertions were made towards cleansing it, although an expenditure of such a trifle as thirty pounds in the employment of a road scraper, drawn by two horses, would have kept it moderately clean and dry; and would have prevented the unnecessary destruction of upwards of three hundred pounds worth of (roadmaking) materials, that were reduced to powder by being soaked and ground, for six months, in water mixed with broken flints.

The only labourers to be seen on the road, during several succeeding months, were those of a neighbouring gentleman, and they were employed in carting the footpath into his enclosures.

By 1818 matters had improved and Redford and Riches in *The History of the Ancient Town of Uxbridge* (1818) observed:

Notwithstanding the numerous acts passed at different periods [for the maintenance of the road], this road till very lately was notoriously bad. It has, however, been much improved within the last three years. In many parts it has been widened, and is now [1818] kept in much better repair than at any former period. We hope the complaints and execrations it has so long excited from wearied and retarded travellers will no longer be justly merited.

The George Inn, Colnbrook. Responsibility for the maintenance of the Bath road from Cranford Bridge to Maidenhead Bridge fell to the Colnbrook Turnpike Trust which seems to have kept its section of the road in a reasonable state of repair. The Trust held its inaugural meeting at the George Inn (*above*) in Colnbrook on 1 June 1727. The first page of the Minute Book records 'the Minutes of a meeting of the Honourable Trustees at The George Inn in Colnbrook, Bucks June 1st 1727 for putting into execution an Act for repairing the road from Cranford Bridge which is in the County of Middlesex to that end of Maidenhead Bridge which is in the County of Bucks'.

Bridges are the most specialised and expensive part of a road to build and maintain, and special conditions governed responsibility for them. When the Turnpike Trusts took over they tried wherever possible to place the responsibility for bridge maintenance on someone else. The Colnbrook Trust had a particular problem because in the 4-mile stretch between Cranford and Colnbrook the Bath Road crosses the Crane and five variously named branches of the River Colne by Longford Bridge, King's Bridge, Moor Bridge, Mad Bridge and Colnbrook Bridge. It managed to relieve itself of the maintenance of four of the six bridges but was left with Cranford Bridge and Colnbrook Bridge.

Colnbrook Bridge over the Colne Brook. This was made of wood in 1543, when Colnbrook was incorporated to maintain it, but the income of the corporation had declined and in 1693 Isaac Bedford, one of the churchwardens, had been obliged to sell the communion plate to pay for the repair of the bridge. In 1729 the Trust tried to get Mr Dee, the bridgemaster, to repair the bridge but again there was no cash. The parish of Stanwell showed that it had no liability and finally, in 1732, the Trust had to accept responsibility. The present bridge was built in 1777, and just here this branch of the Colne forms the boundary between the historic counties of Middlesex and Buckinghamshire. In the middle of the coping of the bridge on either side of the road is a circle divided into quadrants by a straight vertical line and a horizontal wavy line. Around the quadrants is the date 1777, on the western side is the word BUCKS and on its eastern side MIDDX.

Cranford Bridge, *c*. 1910. A bridge at Cranford is marked on Norden's map of Middlesex of 1610; it is known that one existed here before 1274, and that in 1675 the bridge was of wooden construction. In 1764, the Colnbrook Turnpike Trust approached the Countess of Berkeley as Lord of the Manor to repair the bridge. It was rebuilt in three brick arches by Brentford Turnpike Trust in 1776, and the Colnbrook Trust paid them £29 12*s* 0*d* for making up the level of the abutment on the Colnbrook side. The bridge was re-built in 1915 and widened still further in the 1950s (see below).

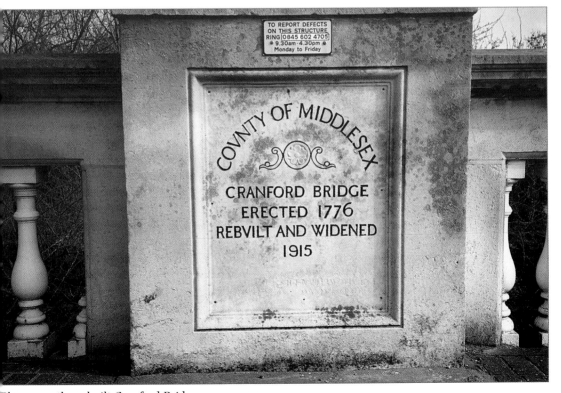

Plaque on the rebuilt Cranford Bridge.

As already discussed the toll-gates on the Uxbridge Road were at Hayes Bridge and between Uxbridge and Hillingdon. The first toll-gate belonging to the Colnbrook Trust was erected opposite the Punchbowl Inn in Colnbrook. The toll-house, demolished about 1960, was a small two-storey building with the words TOLL HOUSE over the door. In 1766 a Toll Board was ordered to be affixed to the toll-gate, showing the tolls laid down in the Act.

Restrictions were imposed on vehicles to protect the road pavement. Extra toll was payable for wagons with wheels narrower than 6in: 25 per cent more for 4–6in wheels and 50 per cent more for wheels narrower than 4.5in. A surcharge was imposed for excess weight, to assess which the Trust had a weighing machine at its gate at Colnbrook, capable of lifting a waggon and its load off the ground. With successive hundredweights overweight the toll became more severe; for example, 3d was charged for the first and second hundredweight overweight; 5s was charged for the 11th and higher hundredweight overweight.

The gatekeepers had to open the gate at any time during the day or night and were vulnerable to thieves and to people who refused to pay the toll. In 1729 two highwaymen seized the gatekeeper, bound him up and stole £2. In 1781 the gatekeeper, Joseph Pierce, was murdered in the night, and the Trust paid his widow a pension of £5 per quarter.

To maintain revenue from the more local traffic a new toll-gate and a small toll house were erected in 1849 at Harlington Corner outside the Coach and Horses.

Toll-gate and toll-house, Harlington Corner, *c.* 1860.

Stagecoach on the Uxbridge Road at Hillingdon, *c.* 1800. Hillingdon church is in the background with the Red Lion on the extreme right. By this time there was a frequent service on both the Uxbridge and the Bath roads. (*K. Pearce*)

Throughout the eighteenth century traffic on the roads continued to increase to the extent shown by a census of traffic on both roads (at Colnbrook and Hanwell) taken in 1835 by the GWR just before it began work on constructing the railway line.

	Colnbrook	**Hanwell**	**Total**
Stagecoaches	77	46	123
Post-chaises and private carriages	105	38	143
Mounted saddle horses	78	27	105
Phaetons and gigs	95	45	140
Spring carts	52	29	81
Stage carts	29	47	76
Waggons	80	52	132
Pigs*	75	NR+	
Sheep*	740	NR+	
Cattle*	110	NR+	

*   *On the hoof*
+   *Not recorded*

Goldsworthy Gurney's Steam Coach. In 1829 Goldsworthy Gurney's steam-powered road vehicle completed the journey from Bath to London at an average speed of 15mph. The project was not a success as breakdowns frequently occurred and the vehicle had a voracious appetite for fuel. However, the main reason for the failure of this and similar ventures was the opposition of the turnpike trusts and the stagecoach companies which joined forces to ensure that steam engines were forced out of business.

Uxbridge Road, Hayes End, c. 1905. The commercial failure of Gurney's steam carriage meant that it was to be nearly eighty years before any more mechanically propelled passenger-carrying vehicles appeared on local roads. The first of these was a tram service along the Uxbridge Road between Shepherd's Bush and Uxbridge which passed through Hayes and Hayes End. This was opened in 1904 and the photograph shows a Route 100 tram of the London United Electric Tramways heading towards Shepherd's Bush. On the left is the Angel public house; the cottages on the right include the Hayes End post office and the police station (just out of the picture). (HHLHS)

Trolleybuses at Hayes End, 1960. The trams along the Uxbridge Road were withdrawn in 1936 and replaced with a trolleybus service. This lasted until 1960 when the trolleybuses were replaced with motor buses. The wheel is set to turn full circle with plans under way to start a tram service along the Uxbridge Road between Shepherds Bush and Uxbridge with twenty trams per hour passing through the town centres of Southall, Hanwell, West Ealing, Ealing and Acton. *(J. Laker)*

Artist's impression of a new tram system on the Uxbridge Road outside Ealing Town Hall. It is intended that the tram will form part of a West London Surface Transport (bus and tram) network with integrated services and ticketing. Memories of the old trams have led to ill-founded criticisms of the project. The trams will run close to the kerb to allow easy access to passengers without impeding other road traffic. *(West London Tram Project)*

The no. 81 bus outside the old Peggy Bedford Hotel at Longford, *c.* 1920. Trams travelled along the Bath Road only between Brentford and Hounslow and motorised buses along the Bath Road from Hounslow did not appear until 1911. Route 81 of the London General Omnibus Company came into service some time after this date and ran from Hounslow to Windsor and it still substantially follows the same course. The type of bus shown in the photograph came into service in 1910 and was withdrawn in 1926. *(WDLHS)*

The former White Hart Inn, Colnbrook. The major relics of the coaching age are the inns at the local stopping places on the Bath Road at Colnbrook and on the Oxford Road at Uxbridge. Colnbrook in particular still retains several of the old coaching inns, instantly recognisable by the archways leading into the coachyards and stabling for horses at the rear of the inns. The former White Hart, the George (page 15) and King John's Palace (page 23) are good examples.

King John's Palace, Colnbrook. The origin of the quaint name for this building is unknown but its appearance gives every indication that it was once a coaching inn. The Star and Garter at the far end is a later eighteenth-century addition, still in use as an inn.

The former King's Arms, Uxbridge High Street, now in use as an employment agency. Uxbridge, being larger than Colnbrook and also an important market town, had even more inns. In 1854 there were fifty-four public houses in the town, of which twenty-four were in the High Street. Although many had long since disappeared, among those that did survive some became victims of the mindless and insensitive re-development of the town that Hillingdon Council instigated in the 1960s. This means that – alas – only two now remain in the High Street, and one of these is no longer in use as an inn.

The Three Tuns, Uxbridge High Street. This is the only coaching inn in Uxbridge High Street that is still in use as an inn and survives in anything like its original form.

Milestone, Bath Road, Harlington. The coaching inns that still remain are the major reminders of the coaching era but other evidence of the Colnbrook Turnpike Trust does exist. In 1741 it erected milestones along the Bath Road, many of which are still in place, notably this one at Harlington Corner.

The Great Western Railway from London to Bristol was opened up as far as Taplow on 4 June 1838; its effect on road traffic was immediate and disastrous. Within two months tolls had fallen to less than a quarter of previous takings, and soon stage and mail coaches were making the journey from Paddington to Taplow on the train. The railway was opened through to Bath and Bristol in June 1841. The last London–Bristol stagecoach ran in October 1843, and the trunk roads were soon left to local traffic. For the next seventy-five years road transport was completely overshadowed by rail.

The Turnpike Trusts had outlived their usefulness, and as their income from traffic declined they were gradually wound up. Responsibility for the trunk roads passed back to the parishes until the re-organisation of local government in the 1880s. County and district councils were established by an 1888 Act of Parliament, when local responsibility for the major roads passed to Middlesex County Council and rural district councils assumed responsibility for the minor roads. From the end of the nineteenth century, however, motorised road traffic expanded exponentially, causing concern about the effect of motor traffic on the roads and demonstrating the need for a better road system. In 1910 a Road Board was set up, financed from taxes on motor vehicles and petrol, but this was disbanded in 1919 and replaced by the Ministry of Transport.

Pump, Bath Road, Colnbrook – another relic of the Turnpike Trust. In 1827 water pumps were installed at intervals along the road to lay the dust and two of these remain on the south side of the old Bath Road. One is outside the Heathrow Park hotel in Longford and the other close to the Punchbowl Inn at Colnbrook. This pump bears a plaque with the inscription 'Erected by order of Beau Nash of Bath 1754'. Apart from the fact that the erection by the Trust is well documented, by 1754 Nash was 80 years old, out of favour, living in poverty, and in no position to order the erection of the pumps. It is quite possible that at an earlier date Nash had been responsible for ensuring that the roads *in* Bath were kept watered to lay the dust and this is how the misconception may have occurred.

Above: Traffic in Brentford High Street (A4). *(Uxbridge Library) Below*: Uxbridge High Street (A40). With the establishment of a central authority with adequate funds to finance road improvements and with the accelerating growth in traffic attention soon turned to the problems caused by traffic on the Bath and Uxbridge roads. This had to pass through towns and villages designed to cater for horse-drawn vehicles. *(K. Pearce)*

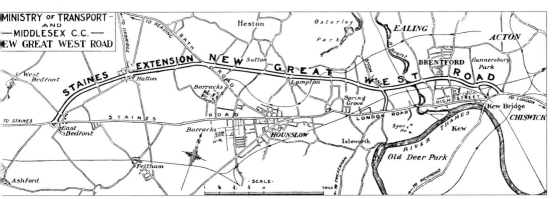

A plan showing the route of the Great West Road. Its construction was started in 1920 and the road was partially opened to traffic in 1925. The solution to problems caused by bottlenecks on the Bath and Uxbridge roads was to bypass both with completely new roads that would pass through what was still open country. The Great West Road, planned as the bypass for the Bath Road, began at Chiswick and crossed the old Bath Road between Hounslow and Cranford where it continued as the Great South West Road as far as Bedfont. The Western Avenue, which bypassed the Uxbridge Road, started at Shepherds Bush and ended at Denham. Work began on the London end in 1921 and continued throughout the 1920s and 1930s but it did not reach Denham until 1943. *(Uxbridge Library)*

The Colnbrook bypass, Longford, 1951. The narrowness of the Bath road through Longford and Colnbrook was a particular bottleneck and we owe its preservation to the Colnbrook bypass, opened in 1928. The patchwork pattern visible on the road was caused by experimental surfacing laid by the Road Research Laboratory, which was initially opened as the Ministry of Transport Experimental Station at the Harmondsworth end of the Colnbrook bypass in 1930.

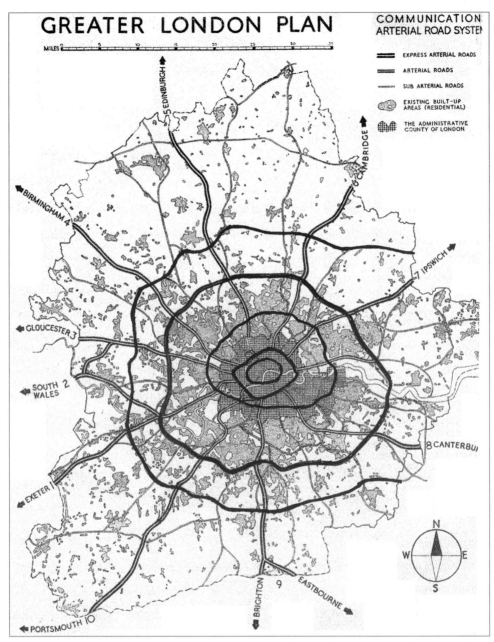

Major road proposals in the Greater London Plan, 1944. The outbreak of war in 1939 brought all but essential road building to an end but did not stop planning for a major postwar road construction programme. The Greater London Plan envisaged a series of concentric ring roads around London which were numbered A to E. The 'E' ring road was a totally new road which later came to fruition as the M25. The 'D' ring road was highly controversial because it passed through built-up areas and its construction would have caused extensive demolitions. The Parkway at Cranford and its extension as the Hayes bypass was the only part of this ever to be built; this passed mostly through open country and was fully opened to traffic in 1991. The 'C' ring road was formed from the North and South Circular roads, a series of existing roads that were connected together so it was largely already in place. The 'A' and 'B' ring roads never appeared because of the massive demolition that their construction would have caused.

The M4 under construction at Harlington, 1964. In addition to the series of circular roads around London the plan envisaged a number of radial roads leading in all directions from the capital. These were later to appear as the motorways leading out from London although they did not follow exactly the same routes that appeared on the plan. Provision for these roads, needed to cope with the growing volume of traffic, was obtained through the Special Roads Act of 1949. This provided for a new type of road, the motorway, from which certain classes of user were to be excluded, and which was designed so that its traffic was not interfered with by that of other roads.

Construction work on the Chiswick–Langley section of the M4 began in the winter of 1962, and the motorway was opened to traffic in 1965. Its construction bisected the district and all the north–south roads had to be diverted to make room for it. The road engineers seemed to go out of their way to maximise its environmental impact. It cut through Boston Manor Park, Osterley Park, Cranford Park and the 'Moats' recreation ground in Harlington. To make matters worse it was, throughout its length, built at ground level when for little if any additional cost it could have been built in a cutting so as to reduce its effect on the locality. The photograph shows the road under construction in the fields between Harlington High Street and Cranford Park, the trees of which can be seen in the distance.

Aerial view, 1961. The photograph shows the area that would soon be cut into three segments by the construction of the M4 motorway and the Airport Spur Road. The junction of the motorway and spur road was to be almost exactly in the middle of the photograph. The southern part of the area, with the village of Sipson in the centre, was still given over to agriculture. To the north-west is the built-up area of West Drayton and in the north-east is the area of Stockley ravaged first by brickworks, then by gravel digging and finally by the uncontrolled tipping of domestic refuse (see later). The railway line and the canal can also be seen in this area running close together and almost parallel to each other.

he M4/Airport Spur Road interchange at West Drayton, *c*. 1990. A comparison of this oblique aerial
iew with the previous aerial photograph shows how badly the area was carved up by the construction
f the motorways and their subsidiary roads. Small portions of land were completely surrounded by
ads making farming impossible and rendering them liable to undesirable developments such as the
onstruction of the grotesque hotel (now the Holiday Inn) to the left of centre.

he Holiday Inn as seen from the Holloway Lane Bridge, 2003. The area of formerly top grade
gricultural land in the foreground was excavated in 1964 to provide material for the construction of
1e M4 and then backfilled with rubbish. Road engineers euphemistically term a feature like this a
orrow-pit', implying that the land will be given back, but this area has stood derelict ever since. The
roposed third runway at Heathrow would pass across this land and would involve the demolition of the
otel – perhaps the only thing that can be said in favour of the runway.

Ceremonial cutting of the first sod on the route of the Hayes bypass, 1985. The ceremony was performed by John McDonnell, then GLC Councillor for Hayes (and MP since 1997). He is seen here (centre) shortly after the ceremony with a group of workmen. The Hayes bypass, together with the Cranford Parkway with which it connects, is all that came to be built of the 'D' ring road of the Greater London Plan. Although the need was obvious and for the most part the route was mostly open land, it was not until 1981 that the then Greater London Council voted by a majority of one to proceed with the project. (J. McDonnell)

John McDonnell standing on the bridge over the Pump Lane interchange shortly before the bypass was opened. The road was formally opened throughout its length from the White Hart at Yeading to the Cranford Parkway by the then Minister of Transport on 29 September 1992. (J. McDonnell)

Above: Station Road, Hayes, early 1980s. Now regarded as Hayes town centre, this part of Hayes was historically the main road through Botwell. The photograph does not reveal the full extent of the traffic congestion – traffic on the left-hand side of the road has been held up by the pedestrian-controlled traffic lights sited outside what was then Payne's shop (now McDonald's), the point from which the photograph was taken. *(J. Hayles)*

Below: Station Road, Hayes, 2003. This photo was taken from the same vantage point as the previous one but some ten years after this part of Station Road had been turned into a cul-de-sac. The opening of the Hayes bypass in 1992 had enabled the town centre to be pedestrianised but surprisingly this did not meet with universal acclaim, particularly from shopkeepers, who complained that it affected their trade. In reality the decline in trade was far more the result of the closure of the factories and the growth in out-of-town shopping centres. To meet such criticism the road has been opened to limited traffic but through access is denied.

The M25, near Heathrow. The 'E' ring road of the Greater London plan came to fruition as the M25, built to link together other motorways around London, and although it is the major motorway link for Heathrow this was the last part to be completed. It was started in 1975 and the final (Heathrow) section of its 120 miles was formally opened by Margaret Thatcher on 29 October 1986. By then it was already becoming a national joke or a disgrace, depending on whether or not one used it. Margaret Thatcher, notorious for lacking any sense either of humour or of proportion, did not see it that way. She boldly declared, 'Some people are saying that the road is too small. Even that it is a disaster. I must say that I cannot stand those who carp and criticise when they ought to be congratulating Britain on a magnificent achievement.'

It had been expected to carry 79,000 vehicles per day by 2001, but within five years it was already carrying more than 200,000 and is the busiest motorway in the country. From time to time plans to widen it have been proposed but have been met with such public hostility that they have had to be scaled down. However, as a result of the decision to construct a fifth terminal at Heathrow, the motorway is to be widened to dual five lanes south of the airport spur junction (14), which will link the terminal to the M25, and dual six lanes between this junction and the junction with the M4 (15).

The route is the national network's most critical strategic point, carrying traffic from the junction with the M3 to the M4 interchange, in addition to thousands of vehicles heading to and from London's main airport, and fleets of lorries travelling between the Channel ports, the West Country and south Wales. Its vulnerability to delays is worsened by the fact that 50 per cent of traffic either joins or leaves along the stretch, resulting in a high level of lane-switching. The widening was originally approved by the Conservative government in 1995, and was denounced as 'madness' by John Prescott, then the opposition transport spokesman. Consequently it was shelved within weeks of Labour's election victory in 1997, but John Prescott, by then the Deputy Prime Minister, later confirmed his madness by accepting the proposal.

2

The Grand Union (Junction) Canal

AN

A C T

For making and maintaining a Navigable Canal from the *Oxford* Canal Navigation, at *Braunston*, in the County of *Northampton*, to join the River *Thames* at or near *Brentford*, in the County of *Middlesex*, and also certain Collateral Cuts from the said intended Canal.

WHEREAS it is practicable to make and maintain a Canal for the Navigation of Boats, Barges, and other Vessels, from the present *Oxford* Canal, in the Parish of *Braunston*, in the County of *Northampton*, through, by, or near the Towns of *Daventry, Newport Pagnell, Leighton Buzzard, Rickmansworth*, and *Uxbridge*, in the several Counties of *Northampton, Buckingham, Bedford, Hertford*, and *Middlesex*, to unite with the River *Thames* at or near *Brentford*, in the said County of *Middlesex*, and also

Preamble.

A   certain

The front page of the Grand Junction Canal Act. The construction of the Grand Junction Canal (now known as the Grand Union Canal) was authorised by Act of Parliament on 30 April 1793. The Act made provision for 'making and maintaining a Navigable Canal from the Oxford Canal navigation at Braunston in the County of Northampton to join the River Thames at, or near, Brentford in the County of Middlesex and also certain collateral cuts from the said canal'. Work on the canal began soon after the passing of the Act, and the Brentford–Uxbridge section was opened on 3 November 1794. *(Uxbridge Library)*

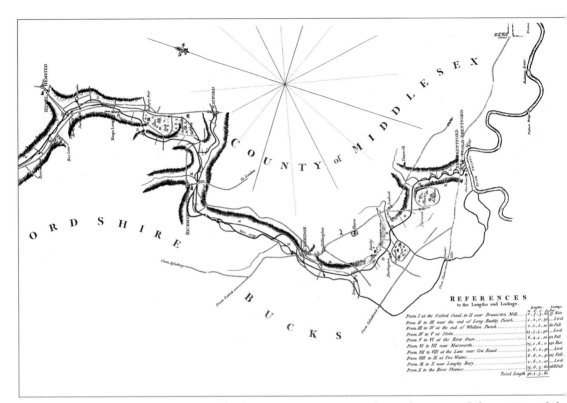

REFERENCES
to the Lengths and Lockage.

From I at the Oxford Canal, to II near Braunston Mill......
From II to III near the end of Long Buckly Parish......
From III to IV at the end of Whitton Parish......
From IV to V at Stoke......
From V to VI at the River Ouse......
From VI to VII near Marsworth......
From VII to VIII at the Lane near Cow Roast......
From VIII to IX at Two Waters......
From IX to X near Langley Bury......
From X to the River Thames......

Total Length 90.1.3.60

The route of the Grand Junction Canal. This contemporary map shows the route of the section of the canal as far north as Hemel Hempstead. The route from Uxbridge to Brentford was completed by 1798 and the link to the Midlands was completed in 1805. A branch running from Bull's Bridge, Hayes to Paddington basin opened in 1801 and the Regent's Canal of 1820 completed the link with the London Docks at the River Lea. In 1882 the 'Slough Arm' link from Cowley connected the canal to Slough and was the last major canal to be built in Britain. In 1929 the Grand Junction Canal and its various connecting links were renamed the Grand Union Canal. (*Uxbridge Library*)

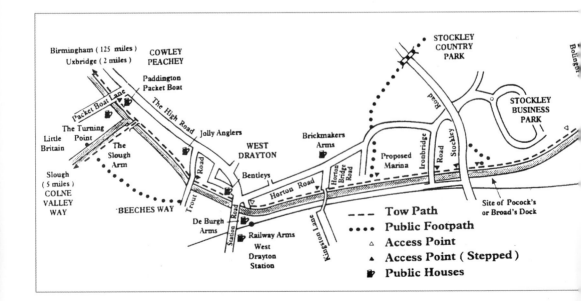

The entrance to Shackle's Dock from the Grand Union Canal, Hayes. The many short branches (docks) of the canal that serviced the brickfields had to be bridged so that access along the tow-path could be maintained. One of the few that remain is this attractive bridge at Shackle's Dock, named after the Shackle family who owned land and brickfields around Hayes. The plaque in the centre of the bridge was affixed in 1994 to mark the 200th anniversary of the opening of the canal through Hayes.

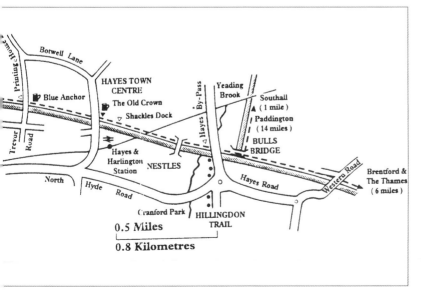

The route of the canal from Cowley to Bull's Bridge, 2003. The canal was once alive with barges carrying bricks, timber, coal and refuse to and from London. Today it is a quiet backwater, with a towpath running its entire length that offers visitors the opportunity to explore and enjoy the area without having to worry about road traffic. (*Map courtesy of the Colne Valley Park Groundwork Trust*).

The Packet Boat from Paddington to Uxbridge on the Grand Junction Canal, 1801 (from Benjamin West's painting with himself and many of his friends on board). For a few years the canal was used for passenger traffic; a guide of 1811 informed travellers that 'at Paddington Basin, a passage boat to Greenford Green and Uxbridge sets off daily at 8.00 a.m. a breakfast is provided on board and other refreshments may be obtained. The terms are reasonable viz. five miles for a shilling, ten miles for eighteen pence and the voyage to Uxbridge may be enjoyed for half-crown.' The service did not prosper as it could not compete with the stagecoach for the serious traveller, but pleasure trips continued until 1853.

Opposite, above: The Grand Union Canal at its junction with the Paddington Branch at Bull's Bridge, looking eastwards along the main branch of the canal. *(P. Sluman)*

Opposite, below: Bull's Bridge, Hayes, showing the junction of the Paddington Branch with the main canal. The signpost in front of the bridge has three arms, pointing respectively to Brentford (6 miles), Paddington (14 miles) and Birmingham (87 miles).

The Paddington Packet Boat, Cowley. The public house stands at the junction of Cowley Road with Packet Boat Lane and still commemorates the name of the packet boat service that ran from Paddington to Uxbridge. The quaint and unusual name has probably ensured that it has avoided the regrettable fashion of brewers to change the long-established names of pubs to something considered more trendy.

Opposite, above: Unloading coal brought by barge to the Nestlé factory, *c.* 1930. At this time nearly all the factories burned coal which for the most part travelled by water from the coalfields to its final destination. Before the arrival of the factories, the gas works at Uxbridge and at Southall had been built close to the canal so that they too could receive coal by water. The canal also led to the establishment of a number of timber yards at Yiewsley and Uxbridge. In the background a train can be seen crossing the railway bridge over the canal. *(HHLHS)*

Opposite, below: Until well into the 1950s coal was the principal fuel used for heating both factories and homes. Most of this coal was brought by water from the coalfields and several coal merchants had their yards adjacent to the canal. The biggest freight company on the Grand Union Canal was Fellows, Morton and Clayton Ltd, and for them the sale of coal was a relatively minor activity. *(Uxbridge Library)*

A 1920s view of the canal with the Cocoa (Nestlé) factory and the railway bridge. *(HHLHS)*

A view from the same position in 2003, with the bridge over Shackle's Dock on the left. *(P. Sluman)*

The canal at Hayes, *c.* 1900. The view is to the east with the bridge over Dawley Road in the background. On the right is the entrance to one of the numerous docks (probably Odell's Dock) that provided access to the brickfields. *(HHLHS)*

A view of the canal from Station Road Bridge, August 2003. Until very recently (see below) the only serious traffic on the canal in the past forty years has been pleasure craft, two of which are seen here. The view is deceptively peaceful since between Hayes and West Drayton the canal is mostly a tree-lined ribbon behind which are many light industrial developments. All of these have turned their backs on the canal and in no way do they rely on it as a means of transport, although this could change.

Canal transport of sand and gravel, West Drayton, 2003. The canal is ideally suited for the transport of large volume, low value materials, where speed is not important provided that a regular supply is maintained. For this reason the canal was used historically for the transport of materials such as coal to the gasworks at Southall and Uxbridge and wood to timber yards at West Drayton and Uxbridge. Such transport had almost completely disappeared, but in 2003 a commercial freight contract, the first in more than thirty years, was devised that would bring sand and gravel from a quarry at Denham to an aggregate depot situated alongside the canal 5 miles away at West Drayton. This was aimed to achieve the transport of 450,000 tonnes of sand and gravel that would otherwise have had to travel by road. The environmental advantages are obvious: two barges per day travelling sedately at 5mph will, over a period of seven years, carry aggregate that would otherwise have had to be conveyed by 45,000 lorry loads. While it is not exactly intensive traffic, amounting to some 64,000 tonnes per annum (or perhaps two or three loaded barges per day), it is nevertheless a step in the right direction. Those inhabitants of Uxbridge, Cowley and West Drayton who would otherwise have to put up with a succession of heavy lorries trundling through their congested streets to the tune of about 130 lorry movements per week, doubtless feel the same. The photograph taken in August 2003 shows one of the barges after it had discharged its load, with the aggregate depot in the background.

3

The Railway

The Act to permit the Great Western Railway Company to construct a line between London and Bristol, which would pass through West Drayton and Hayes, was finally approved by Parliament in 1835. Many objections were raised to its construction: it was argued that the GWR was neither 'Great' nor 'Western' or even a railway at all. Others objected on the grounds that it would poison the air; or that it would deprive the Thames of its traffic so causing the river to become choked; and, most ridiculous of all, that it would corrupt the morals of the boys of Eton College by giving them easy access to the dissipations of London.

Work soon started on its construction and West Drayton station was the first to open on the line from Paddington. The whole route from Paddington to Taplow was opened to passengers on 4 June 1838. By 1840 this had been extended as far as Reading and the line to Bristol opened on 30 June 1841.

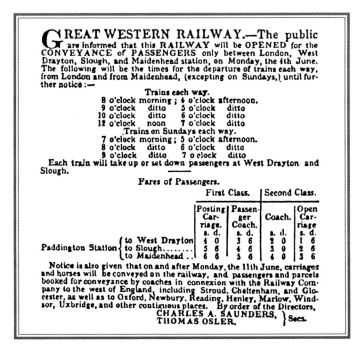

An announcement in *The Times*, 2 June 1838. At this time the bridge over the Thames at Maidenhead had not been completed, and despite what the announcement suggests the line ran only as far as Taplow. On the same day the Eton College authorities applied for an injunction to prevent trains from stopping at Slough. It was dismissed on the grounds that stopping did not violate the condition that a station was not to be provided at Slough! (*Uxbridge Library*)

Great Western Railway.
LONDON TO MAIDENHEAD.

On and after the 1st of May, the SOUTHALL STATION will be opened
For Passengers and Parcels.

An **Extra Train** to **Slough** will leave Paddington on **Sunday Mornings**, at **half-past 9 o'clock**, calling at Ealing, Hanwell, Southall and West Drayton.

Horses and Carriages, being at the Paddington or Maidenhead Station ten minutes before the departure of a Train, will be conveyed upon this Railway.

Charge for 4-wheel Carriage, 12s. Two-wheel ditto, 8s. For 1 Horse, 10s. Pair of Horses, 16s.

Post Horses are kept in readiness both at Paddington and Maidenhead, and upon sufficient notice being given at Paddington, or at the Bull and Mouth Office, St. Martin's-le Grand, would be sent to bring Carriages from any part of London to the station, at a moderate charge.

TRAINS.

From Paddington To Maidenhead.		From Maidenhead To Paddington.	
		6 o'clock morning, calling at - - Slough	
		(and on Wednesday Morning at Southall)	
8 o'clock morn. calling at - Southall and Slough		**8** do. - Slough and West Drayton	
9 do. - - - Slough		**9** do. - Slough and West Drayton	
10 do. - West Drayton and Slough		**10** do. - - Slough and Southall	
12 do. - West Drayton and Slough		**12** do. - Slough and West Drayton	
2 o'clock afternoon - West Drayton and Slough		**2** o'clock afternoon - - Slough and Southall	
4 do. - - - Slough		**4** do. - - - Slough	
5 do. - Hanwell and Slough		**5** do. - Slough and Hanwell	
6 o'clock evening Ealing, West Drayton and Slough		**6** o'clock evening - Slough and West Drayton	
7 do. - Southall and Slough		**7** do. - Slough and Ealing	
8 do. - - Slough			

The six o'clock up Train will call at Southall on Wednesday mornings, for the convenience of persons attending the market on that day.

SHORT TRAINS.

From Paddington To West Drayton.		From West Drayton To Paddington.	
½ past **9** o'Clock Morning,		½ before **9** o'Clock Morning,	
½ past **1** do. Afternoon, calling at { Ealing, Hanwell, AND Southall,		½ before **11** do. calling at { Southall, Hanwell, AND Ealing.	
½ past **4** do. do.		½ before **3** Afternoon	
½ past **8** do. Evening		½ before **7** o'Clock Evening	

☞ *There are no second class close carriages in the short Trains.*

Passengers and Parcels for Slough and Maidenhead will be conveyed from all the stations by means of the short Trains, waiting to be taken on by the succeeding long Train, as above; and in like manner they will be conveyed from Maidenhead and Slough, to every station on the Line.

On SUNDAYS,

From Paddington To Maidenhead.			From Maidenhead To Paddington.		
8 o'clock Morn, calling at - - Ealing and Slough			**6** o'clock morn. calling at - - - Slough		
½ past **8** do. do. - West Drayton and Slough			**8** do. do. - Slough Southall and Ealing		
9 do. do. - Southall and Slough			**9** do. do. Slough West Drayton and Hanwell		
5 afternoon do. Hanwell West Drayton and Slough			**5** afternoon do. - - Slough and Hanwell		
6 evening do. Ealing West Drayton and Slough			**6** evening do. - Slough and West Drayton		
7 do. do. - Southall and Slough			**7** do. do. - - Slough and Ealing		

SHORT TRAINS,
PADDINGTON TO SLOUGH.

Half-past Nine o'Clock Morning, - - - calling at Ealing, Hanwell, Southall, and Drayton.

To West Drayton.		From West Drayton.	
½ past **9** o'Clock Morning, calling at { Ealing, Hanwell, & Southall. and proceeding to Slough		½ before **8** o'Clock Morning, calling at { Southall, Hanwell & Ealing.	
½ past **8** do. Evening, Ealing, Hanwell & Southall		½ before **7** do. Evening,	

FARES.

Paddington.	1st. Class. Coach.	Second Class. Close.	Second Class. Open.	Maidenhead.	1st. Class. Coach.	Second Class. Close.	Second Class. Open.
To Ealing	1 6	1 0	0 9	To Slough	2 0	1 6	1 0
Hanwell ...	2 0	1 6	1 0	West Drayton	3 0	2 6	2 0
Southall	2 6	1 9	1 3	Southall	4 0	3 0	2 6
West Drayton	3 6	2 0	1 6	Hanwell ...	4 6	3 6	3 0
Slough	4 6	3 0	2 6	Ealing	5 0	4 0	3 6
Maidenhead.	5 6	4 0	3 6	Paddington.	5 6	4 0	3 6

The same Fares will be charged from Slough to West Drayton as from Maidenhead to Slough.

OMNIBUSES and Coaches start from Princes Street, Bank, one hour before the departure of each Train, calling at the Angel Inn, Islington; Bull Inn, Holborn; Moore's Green Man and Still, Oxford Street; Golden Cross, Charing Cross; Chaplin's Universal Office, Regent Circus; and Gloucester Warehouse, Oxford Street; to the Paddington station.—**Fare 6d.** without Luggage.

A GWR timetable of 1839 published to announce the opening of Southall station. By then the bridge across the Thames had been completed, and trains really did run as far as Maidenhead, not just to Taplow as had hitherto been the case.

Line drawing of the Vulcan steam engine. This was one of the first two locomotives to run on the GWR line from Paddington to Taplow. The Vulcan and another engine, the Premier, were transported in 1837 by canal from the London Docks to West Drayton where they were lifted from the barge and taken to nearby West Drayton station. The Vulcan became the first engine to use the newly constructed railway line when it was tried out on the tracks during the following weeks. *(WDLHS)*

The GWR station at West Drayton looking towards Hayes, 1897. The station was built in 1879 to replace the 1838 original, which had been built about a quarter-mile to the west. Today numerous buses link the station with the surrounding area. In 1897 the only access to the station was by horse-drawn transport and two carriages are waiting in the forecourt to pick up passengers from the trains. *(J. Skinner)*

Locomotive *Goodrich Castle* from Paddington passing through West Drayton station, 5 July 1962. At this time the station was still a junction for the branch lines to Uxbridge and Staines, which had been opened in 1856 and 1884 respectively. These lines were closed in the 1960s as part of the notorious cuts made by Dr Beeching, the then chairman of British Rail. *(R. Smith)*

West Drayton station, *c.* 1980. The station has changed little in appearance since it was built in 1879, and looks much the same today except that the building on the right of the photograph has since been demolished. *(Copyright Mrs. J.E. Goode)*

Two views of Hayes station, *c.* 1914, looking towards Southall. Officially known as Hayes and Harlington station, it was opened in 1864 some twenty-five years after the neighbouring stations at Southall and West Drayton. The wide spacing between the tracks is a relic of the GWR's original broad gauge (7ft) which was altered in 1892 to the standard gauge used by all the other railway companies. In the background of the upper photograph Sandow's Cocoa and Chocolate factory (now part of Nestlé) is under construction (see Chapter 6). *(HHLHS)*

Another early view of Hayes station, looking back to Station Road, *c.* 1910. The station was completely re-modelled in the 1930s when the bridge was widened and the road re-aligned. *(HHLHS)*

A 95 bus on Hayes station bridge, 1931. The bridge was rebuilt and the road re-aligned in the mid-1930s. Before this the road south from the station had not been linked to North Hyde Road at the present-day traffic lights, but had met North Hyde Road further east by the road now known as Old Station Road. *(HHLHS)*

A view from
Hayes station
bridge looking
towards
Harlington,
c. 1930.
(HHLHS)

The funeral train of George VI passing through Hayes in 1952. Ever since the death of Queen Victoria in 1901 the body of the reigning monarch has been taken through Hayes and West Drayton by train from London to Windsor. This photograph shows the train steaming west towards Bourne's Bridge with the EMI factories in the background. *(Uxbridge Library)*

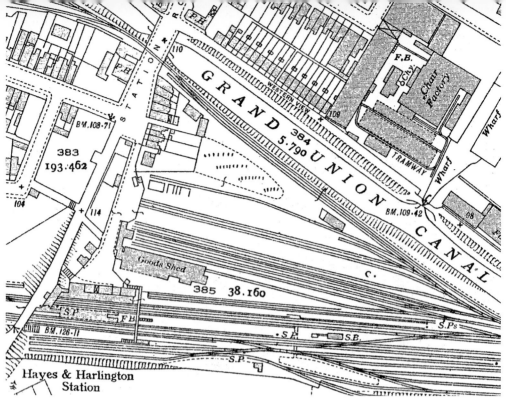

383
193·462

104

114

Goods Shed

385 38·160

Hayes & Harlington
Station

Above: Hayes station and environs, 1935. *Below:* Hayes goods yard, 1997. Apart from carrying the main lines between Paddington and the West Country, Hayes station had a large goods yard and also a direct rail link (across Station Road via a level-crossing – see page 104) to the factories on the opposite side of the road. With the decline of manufacturing industry and the growth of road traffic, the goods yard is now completely redundant, as can be seen in the lower photograph. This leaves a large triangle of land between the main line, the canal and Station Road that is ripe for re-development. It is particularly well placed because Hayes station already has a good service to Paddington, it could become a stop for the Heathrow Express and it is on the route of the proposed Crossrail project that would link Paddington and Liverpool Street stations by means of a new deep tunnel. If built, Crossrail would revolutionise east–west traffic across London and give the capital something similar to what Paris has had since 1965. The likely cost is between £10 and £15 billion, i.e. comparable to the cost of the ill-conceived Concorde project but far more useful.

A 45 bus standing outside Hounslow Barracks station, 1912. The district's nearest and first link with the London Underground system was the extension in 1884 of the District Line to a station on the Bath Road at Hounslow, to serve Hounslow Barracks. The station was renamed Hounslow West in December 1925. The small building seen on the right was replaced by the present-day station in 1931 and the Piccadilly Line was introduced on to the route. *(G. Smeed)*

Hatton Cross station. This was the first station to be opened on the extension to the Piccadilly Line from Hounslow West, constructed to help relieve road congestion to the airport. The route to the central terminal area was completed in 1976. The Piccadilly Line extension has had little adverse environmental effect as the line runs underground for almost its entire length. The line provides direct access to central London with a travelling time of 45 minutes; unfortunately the trains are not suited to the carriage of passengers with a large amount of luggage nor can they be adapted.

A temporary viaduct over Shepiston Lane to allow construction of the Paddington–Heathrow rail link to proceed, August 1995. The link to the main line at Hayes was originally to have been above ground, passing over the M4 on a 18ft-high viaduct, and gradually coming down to ground level before going underground to the airport centre. The photograph gives some indication of how intrusive this would have been. The plan was rejected on environmental grounds and most of the link was eventually built in a tunnel.

One of the Heathrow Express trains that provide a non-stop link between the airport and Paddington with a journey time of 15 minutes. *(Photo courtesy of Heathrow Express plc)*

4

Aviation

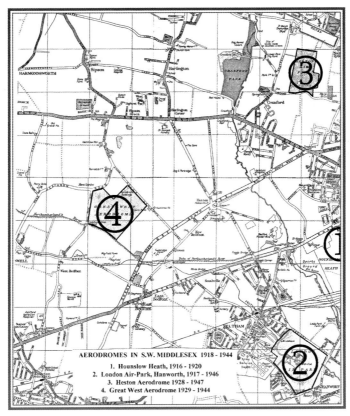

AERODROMES IN S.W. MIDDLESEX 1918 - 1944

1. Hounslow Heath, 1916 - 1920
2. London Air-Park, Hanworth, 1917 - 1946
3. Heston Aerodrome 1928 - 1947
4. Great West Aerodrome 1929 - 1944

West Middlesex was the natural choice for airfields by virtue of its proximity to London, its good communications, a flat landscape and (at the time) a relatively low population density. In the 1920s four aerodromes were established within a few miles of each other. All were privately owned, none had concrete runways and initially they were not particularly important because Croydon was then the main airport for London. In the early 1930s it was decided that Heston (3) should become the major airport for London; this would have come to pass but for the outbreak of war in 1939. However, the war gave the Air Ministry the opportunity to requisition the Fairey airfield at Heathrow (4) and its surrounding land under the pretext that it was urgently needed as a base for the RAF. This development was no less than a conspiracy against the public interest: it took place on some of the finest agricultural land in the country, which was under intensive cultivation and growing food at a time when there were severe shortages. The Defence of the Realm Act 1939 was passed so as to allow the authorities to requisition land without the need to go to Public Inquiry, in pursuance of the genuine need to use all resources to be given over to fighting the war. It should not have been used to requisition land for a civil airport under the pretext it was needed by the RAF.

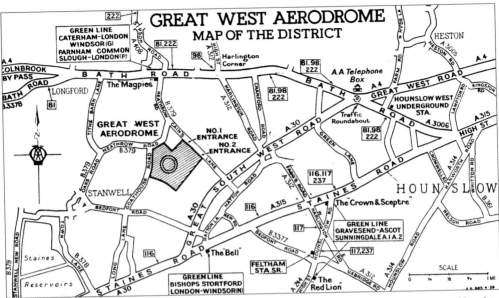

Between 1929 and 1939 the Fairey Aviation Company of Hayes acquired 240 acres of land in Cains Lane, Heathrow, as an aerodrome to test its aircraft. From 1935 to 1939 the aerodrome was the location of the Annual Garden Party of the Royal Aeronautical Society and the map shown above is taken from the 1939 programme. *(J. Marshall)*

A prototype Fairey Battle bomber flying over the aerodrome in 1936. Fairey's hangar can be seen immediately under the propeller of the aeroplane. Until the outbreak of war this was the only building on the airfield, which had no concrete runways. The road running diagonally across the foreground is Cains Lane and the view is to the north. *(Photograph by Charles Brown in March 1936, courtesy of RAF Museum, reference no. P102705)*

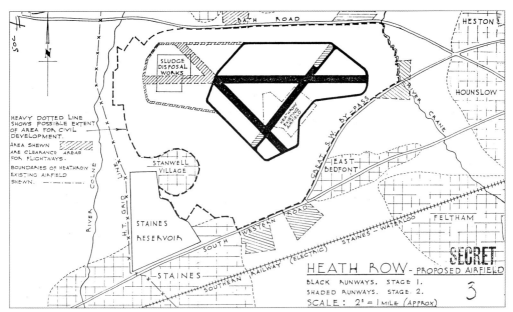

Initial plans for an airfield at Heathrow, drawn up by the Air Ministry in 1943. Because of problems with finding an alternative site for the sludge works the plan had to be modified so that for the next sixty years the works would remain as an enclave sandwiched between the two main E–W runways. The airport's construction began in May 1944. By the following May the war in Europe had ended and the airfield was never used by the RAF. (*PRO File AVIA 2/2269*)

A Hawker Tempest fighter flying over Heathrow in the summer of 1945. The airport can be seen to be taking shape with the northern E–W runway virtually completed. The view is to the east with the Bath Road towards the left edge of the photograph. The ugly scar on the landscape caused by the airport had not yet started to encroach on the surrounding area but like all cancerous growths it soon would. (*Reproduced by permission from the Michael Stroud collection*)

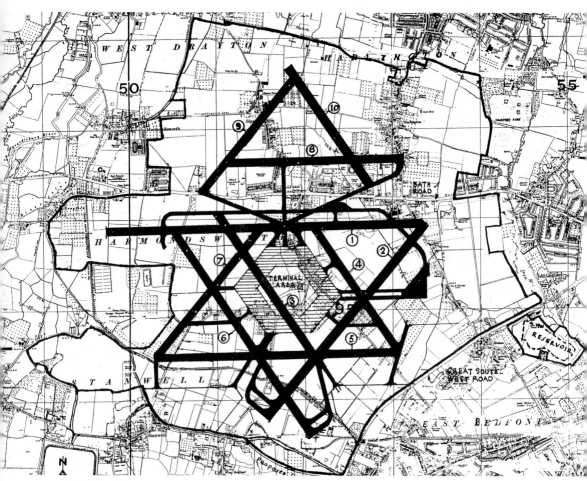

Flushed with their success in establishing under false pretences a civil airport at Heathrow the aviation lobby became increasingly ambitious and in 1946 secured approval to extend the airport to the north of the Bath Road. The map shows the proposals, which involved the construction as planned of the airport to the south of the Bath Road – to be followed by an extension that would have involved the complete destruction of Sipson and Harlington. The plan was modified in 1951 so that 'only' the southern half of Sipson and Harlington would have been demolished, and instead Harmondsworth would have been obliterated. The plans were abandoned in December 1952, not because of the environmental effects, but because of the economic costs. Undismayed, aviation interests have continued ever since to press for the extension of the airport with the construction of a third E–W runway. *(PRO File AIR19/388)*

Heathrow airport, 1954. The area to the south of the Bath Road had by then been completely overwhelmed but to the north the villages of Harmondsworth (in the right-hand corner of the photograph) and of Sipson (centre left) were still relatively undisturbed. If a third runway were to be built at Heathrow the whole area seen in this photograph would be occupied by the airport. (*J. Marshall*)

Heathrow airport, early 1990s. These aerial views show the airport soon after the fourth terminal had been opened at the south-east edge of the airport. The Perry Oaks sludge works was then still an enclave between the two main E–W runways but was destined to become the site of a fifth terminal despite the firm commitment made by BAA at the fourth terminal inquiry that it would not seek to extend the airport any further. *(BAA plc)*

Heathrow Airport

❶ Terminal 1 ❻ Control Tower
❷ Terminal 2 ❼ Maintenance Area
❸ Terminal 3 ❽ Cargo Area
❹ Terminal 4
❺ Perry Oaks Sludge Works proposed
   site of Terminal 5

HEATHROW AIRPORT DEVELOPMENT

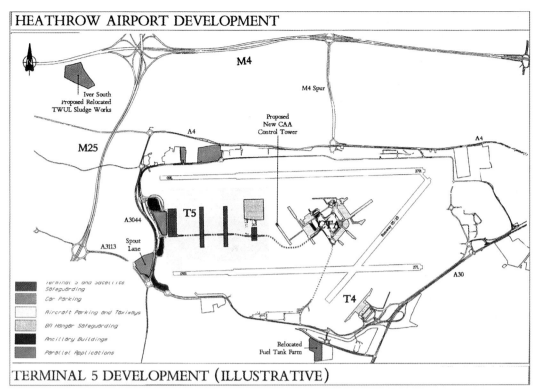

TERMINAL 5 DEVELOPMENT (ILLUSTRATIVE)

Although at the Fourth Terminal Inquiry BAA claimed that it would not be seeking any further development at Heathrow, in 1992 the company submitted a planning application for a fifth terminal. The plan proposed relocating the Perry Oaks sludge works and developing the site as the fifth terminal connected by a link road to the M25. The terminal was aimed to cater for an additional 30 million passengers per year on top of the 50 million at the 1992 level of use. As the histogram below shows, the terminal on its own would when opened be larger than any other UK airport apart from the existing Heathrow. *(Evidence to T5 Inquiry)*

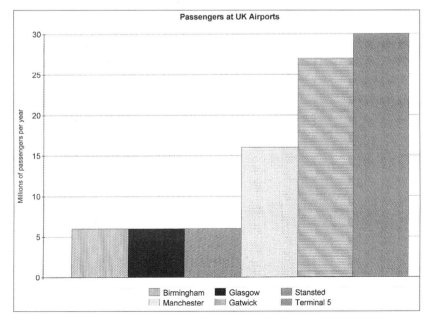

A histogram prepared from figures provided by BAA at the Terminal 5 Inquiry, showing passenger numbers at existing airports in 1997 and the projected figures for Terminal 5.

Artist's impression of Terminal 5 and its link with the M25. The link with the M25 is to be by a completely new spur road which, according to BAA, will be 'sensitively landscaped and blend seamlessly with the Colne Valley [*sic*])'. The view is highly idealised and in reality it is all too likely that the land around the roads will assume the appearance of so much land around the airport, with its car parks, breakers' yards, etc. *(BAA plc)*

Opposite, above: Artist's impression of the Terminal 5 building. BAA anticipated that the terminal would be opened by 2001 but there was immense local opposition on an unprecedented scale. As a result the Public Inquiry into the proposal lasted four years (the longest ever) and it is not expected that the terminal will become operational until 2007. *(BAA plc)*

Opposite, below: Artist's impression of a bird's-eye view of the Terminal 5 complex and its links to the M25.

Planning permission for a fifth terminal was granted in 2001 and construction started soon after – five years later than originally anticipated. The area of land involved was not just confined to the site of the Perry Oaks sludge works but stretched far beyond, including areas that were not primarily to be occupied by the terminal. The area shown above was part of the Bedfont Court estate, just to the west of Perry Oaks, which had been developed by Middlesex County Council as an area of smallholdings, each with its own bungalow and small plot of land, for occupation by ex-servicemen after the First World War. This, as the photograph shows, survived as a surprisingly rural area until it was acquired by BAA, when most of the site was used to provide gravel for the construction of the fifth terminal. The lower photograph shows preliminary clearance of the part of the site that was to be occupied by the T5 complex. (*Above: R.McManus*)

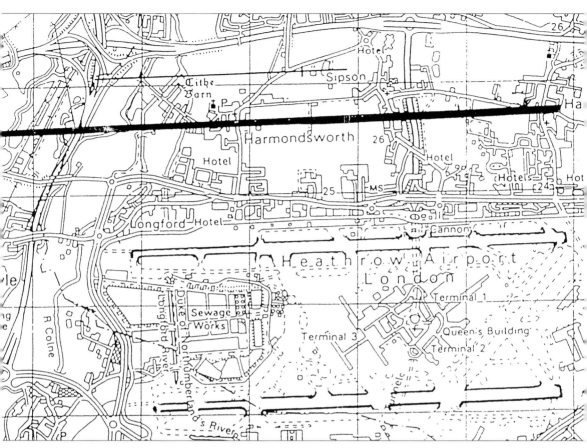

In 1990 the Government appointed a Working Group on Runway Capacity in the South East (RUCATSE) to find sites for additional runway capacity. The Committee came up with the proposal that the construction of a third runway at Heathrow should be a strong contender and the map shown above is taken from its deliberations. The Committee estimated the environmental effects of its proposals (see below), but although these were horrific it still considered that Heathrow was the best option. The Government at the time rejected the proposals but this did not deter the aviation lobby, which behind the scenes continued to press for the construction of a third runway.

For example, at about the same time British Airways applied for planning permission to construct what it termed its Corporate Business Centre on 5.3ha (13 acres) of green-belt land on Harmondsworth Moor. In return it agreed to rehabilitate the remaining 104ha (257 acres) of the Moor and lay this out as public parkland to be known as Prospect Park. The report of the inquiry into this application was published in October 1992 and the Inspector recommended that it should be approved. He dismissed as conjectural the possibility that the park would be engulfed by a third runway but subsequent events have shown that this is a distinct possibility. British Airways is a most improbable public benefactor and even at the time only the most gullible would believe that it did not at least have this possibility in mind. Since then fresh proposals have been made for the construction of a third runway with British Airways well to the fore (p. 68) in the clamour for this from members of the aviation lobby. (*RUCATSE Report*)

EFFECTS OF A THIRD RUNWAY
(RUCATSE REPORT 1993)

Demolitions:

Houses	3300
Listed buildings	44
Public Buildings	11
Hotels	10
Other commercial	15,000
	(m² floorspace)

Land-take for enlargement (hectares):

Area of existing airport	1197
Area of enlarged airport	1862
Total land-take	665
Green belt	602
of which:	
Grade 1 Land	427
Other agricultural	22
Recreational	59

Additional land-take for relocations 1500ha. (6 square miles)

Acquisition/relocation costs	£1162m (1992 prices)
Total construction costs	£3271m

a) British Airways is committed to being a good neighbour, concerned for the community and environment. We continually strive to improve our social and environmental performance, with the objective of ensuring that our activities contribute to the sustainable development of the communities in which we operate.

b) British Airways is supporting the development of an additional, short runway at Heathrow. We believe that a third Heathrow runway is consistent with the principles of sustainable development as long as measures are taken to reduce adverse environmental and local impacts.

(Excerpts from British Airways' Social and Environmental Report for 2002/2003)

'Doublethink, the power of holding two contradictory beliefs simultaneously and accepting both of them.'   *(George Orwell, 1984)*

HEATHROW*news*

FEBRUARY 1995   THIS NEWSPAPER IS PRODUCED FOR LOCAL RESIDENTS BY HEATHROW AIRPORT LIMITED

THIRD RUNWAY RULED OUT

Government backs BAA in ditching third runway possibility

News & Advertising 01895 451000 ⬚ Classified 01895 451027   c   Wednesday, January 13, 1999   THE LEADER   Page 25

HEATHROW*news*

JANUARY 1999

THESE TWO PAGES HAVE BEEN PAID FOR BY BAA HEATHROW TO INFORM READERS OF THE LATEST DEVELOPMENTS IN THE TERMINAL 5 INQUIRY

RULE OUT THIRD RUNWAY SAYS BAA

At every public inquiry into proposals for extending Heathrow BAA has claimed that it would not seek any further development. This claim has proved to be false on every single occasion. During the Fifth Terminal Inquiry, as can be seen from the headlines of two editions of the company news-sheet, it reiterated that it did not wish for a third runway. The edition of 13 January 1999 claimed that 'We don't want to build a third runway at Heathrow and Terminal 5 will not lead to a third runway. But some people simply don't accept this and have caused confusion and worry by claiming that we have a hidden agenda. Well we haven't and we are very concerned to put people's minds at rest on this issue.' BAA's attitude was later criticised by a Parliamentary Committee on aviation which considered that 'At best the company was culpably short-sighted when it told the Terminal 5 inquiry that an extra runway at Heathrow would be unacceptable for environmental reasons; at worst it was wilfully misleading'.

Although the government of the day rejected the RUCATSE proposals the Department for Transport (DfT) continued with consultations as to how the expected demand for air travel could be met. It arrived at its estimates by projecting into the next thirty years the growth encountered in the previous thirty years and this showed that air travel would triple between 2000 and 2030. Taken at face value these forecasts show that by 2030 demand would be growing at the rate of a new Gatwick every eighteen months or a new Heathrow every three years. Despite the absurdity of these predictions the DfT published a series of consultation papers in 2003 which outlined several options. One of these was a 'short' 2000m runway at Heathrow to run between the A4 and the M4 parallel to the two existing E–W runways. This, of course is what the aviation lobby had been working towards for the last sixty years. BAA, which was on record as being totally opposed to a third

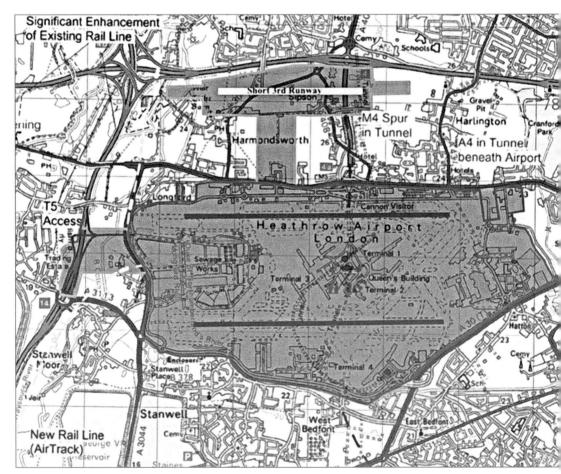

The position of a possible third runway at Heathrow. The grey area represents the extent of the expande airport with the new runway linked to the existing airport, leaving what was left of Harmondsworth an Sipson to be sandwiched between the runways. Because of this the consultation paper claimed tha 'only' 260 houses needed to be demolished although it did accept that the historic centre c Harmondsworth village, including the church and the Great Barn, could not survive. (From The Futur Development of Transport in the United Kingdom: South East, Department for Transport 2003)

runway (see above), and earlier had claimed that it did not want a fifth terminal, quickly seized the opportunity and presented plans to include an additional terminal between the existing northern runway and the new 'short' runway.

Following the consultation exercise the Government published its White Paper, *The Future of Air Transport*, in December 2003. This made it abundantly clear that the consultation exercise was a complete sham and that the decision to expand Heathrow had been made well before the exercise had even begun. All the public protests had been in vain but the aviation lobby was thwarted, at least temporarily, by an unexpected obstacle. For the first time ever it was told 'You can't have it now', although it was told that if it behaved its wishes might eventually be granted.

The reason why the government could not comply with the aviation industry's demands was because the government was bound by law to comply with the mandatory air quality limit values for nitrogen oxides laid down by a European Union Directive on air quality that would come into force in 2010. The Heathrow area already exceeded these limits and estimates showed that the construction of a third runway would mean that 35,000 people would be exposed to nitrogen oxide concentrations above the legal limit. The government therefore had to concede that it could only support the construction of a third runway at Heathrow if the key conditions relating to compliance with air quality limits can be met. It estimated that although there was no immediate prospect of this there was a substantially better prospect of achieving it if the construction of a third runway were delayed until 2015–20. By this time it hoped that steps taken in the intervening period to reduce pollution would have produced the desired effect. This meant that the shadow that had been hanging over the villages to the north of Heathrow for more than fifty years was due to last for at least another twelve.

Contrasting headlines from the editions of the *Uxbridge Gazette* of 19 December 1952 and 17 December 2003. The first celebrates the end of the first attempt to construct a third runway at Heathrow. The celebrations were premature; who would then have thought that the aviation industry would be so persistent in its demands for the expansion of Heathrow that almost fifty-one years to the day later it would still be pressing for expansion.

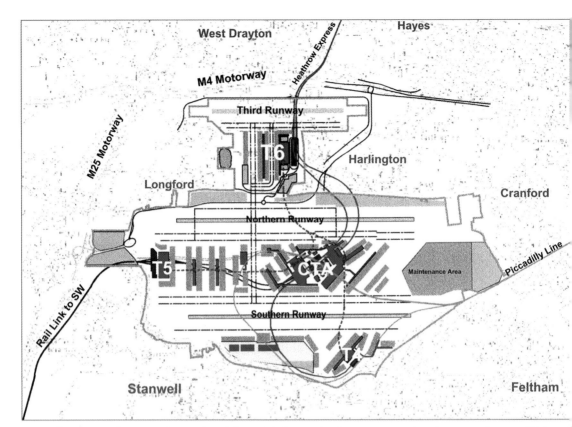

One of a series of proposals produced by BAA for a third runway at Heathrow with an additional terminal (T6). This was produced in 2003, only four years after BAA had repeatedly claimed at the fifth terminal inquiry that 'We don't want to build a third runway at Heathrow and Terminal 5 will not lead to a third runway'. The result of the Inquiry was, of course, a foregone conclusion, although in recommending that the planning application should be approved, the Chairman of the Inquiry went on to say, 'I agree with BAA that the evidence placed before me demonstrates that a third main runway at Heathrow would have such severe and widespread impacts on the environment as to be totally unacceptable.' This was reiterating BAA's own evidence at the Inquiry and in support BAA issued an announcement in *Heathrow News* (see earlier) to this effect. This was accompanied by a letter sent personally to everybody living in the vicinity of the airport by Mike Roberts, the then Managing Director of Heathrow Airport, in which he said 'I'd like to reassure you that they [i.e. the T5 proposals] will *not* require another runway or an increase in night flights' (his emphasis).

BAA had claimed that it was not working to a hidden agenda but lost no time in producing plans for expansion far beyond that proposed by the Government. These involved not just a third runway but an additional terminal (Terminal 6) to cater for the additional traffic movements. The proposals would involve the total demolition of Sipson and 700 houses but still assumed that what was left of Harmondsworth and Harlington would remain between the runways, even though they would be completely uninhabitable. (*BAA plc*)

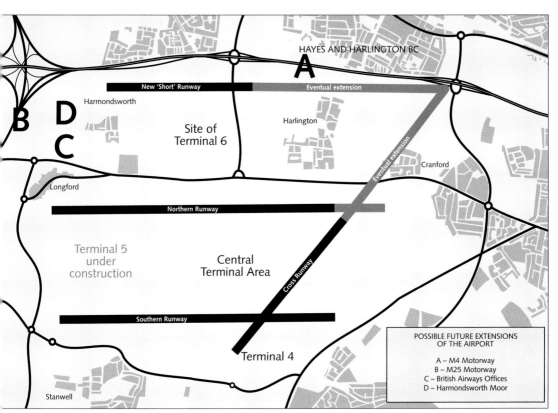

As already mentioned every major development at Heathrow has been accompanied by an assurance from BAA (and its predecessors) that it had no further territorial demands. In every single case, as soon as planning permission was granted, BAA went back on its word and asked for a further extension. It is not therefore difficult to predict with a considerable degree of certainty that if permission were to be granted for the construction of a 'short' third runway it would be followed soon after by an application to extend it eastwards to make it the same length as the two existing E–W runways. The map shows the ease with which this could be achieved and how easy it would be, once this was in place, to extend the existing cross runway to turn Heathrow into an airport with four main runways. This is the goal to which the aviation industry has been working for the past sixty years.

Harmondsworth village is a flourishing community with the ancient parish church still acting as the focal point for the village. For more than 1,000 years the graveyard attached to the church has been used for the burial of the villagers and, uniquely for the area, it is still in use for this purpose. If the aviation industry has little respect for the living residents of Harmondsworth it can hardly be expected to have any at all for the dead, and the third runway would involve the desecration of the churchyard. The photograph shows a protest demonstration held in October 2002 by villagers with relatives buried in the churchyard.

Opposite, above: The view from the top of St Mary's Church, Harmondsworth. In the immediate foreground is Manor Farm, a Grade II listed building dating from the early nineteenth century; this and the church would be engulfed if a third runway were to be built. In the distance are the buildings of British Airways' head office, known as Waterside. British Airways gained planning permission for this to be built on green-belt land in return for agreeing to lay out the surrounding Harmondsworth Moor as a public park. It is unlikely that the prospect of the park being engulfed by a third runway had escaped the notice of British Airways, which is possibly why the name initially chosen for the park by BA was Prospect Park.

Opposite, below: Harmondsworth from the M4. The twelfth-century church is in the middle of the photograph, with the Great Barn (Grade I listed and a Scheduled Ancient Monument) to its right. A third runway at Heathrow would run across the foreground of this photograph and lead to the demolition of the church, barn and historic village centre.

A protest meeting in Harmondsworth village, 7 June 2003, one of a large number of such meetings. If a third runway were to be built Harmondsworth would be obliterated.

Opposite, above: A carol service in the Great Barn, 13 December 2003. The threat to Harmondsworth has had the effect of uniting villagers in the fight to save their village. One way of showing their solidarity has been a carol service in the Great Barn that has become an annual event since the expansion of Heathrow was first announced. The long exposure required for the photograph has meant that the people are rather blurred but the magnificent fifteenth-century interior of the barn is shown to good effect. *(D. McCartney)*

Opposite, below: Aircraft coming in to land over Cranford. This shows that the situation for people living under flight paths close to Heathrow is already intolerable but more people than ever before are affected by aircraft noise. Some areas are subjected to a plane coming overhead once every 90 seconds from 6 in the morning until after 10 at night. Over a million people in London and the Thames Valley live under the Heathrow flight path; it extends from Greenwich and Eltham in the east to Windsor and Henley in the west and as far north as Brent, Finsbury Park and Mile End. Of this number it is officially accepted that 307,000 are very badly affected. If a third runway were to be built the situation would become even worse.

Local residents are not the only people adversely affected by aircraft noise. Areas of very high amenity value which attract many tourists are also on the Heathrow flight paths. These include Kew Gardens *(above)* and Osterley Park *(below)*, to which might be added Windsor, Hampton Court, Syon House and Richmond Park.

5

Brick-making &
Gravel Extraction

Much of the area to the south of the Uxbridge Road lies over gravel beds created by the changing course of the River Thames as it gradually moved southwards after the last Ice Age. The gravel beds are covered by a variable thickness of brick-earth and both layers have been extensively exploited to provide materials for the building industry. To a limited extent gravel extraction and brick-making must have been carried out since the settlements were first established but in the mid-nineteenth century the growth of London, the presence of brick-making material and the ready means of transporting the bricks by canal to the metropolis led to a large area of land close to the canal between Yiewsley and Hayes being given over to brickworks centred on Starveall (later renamed Stockley), Dawley, Botwell and Yeading. Thorne, in his *Handbook to the Environs of London* (1876) remarked of the area around West Drayton: 'The country is level but there are shady lanes and broad green meadows though sulphurous and manury smells from brickfields, canal and wharves somewhat interfere with the sense of enjoyment.'

As the brick-earth became exhausted the underlying gravel was later exploited and then the large holes left by the excavations were filled with London's rubbish brought by canal. This was dumped indiscriminately with the result that the whole area became derelict and resembled a lunar landscape. For many years the high agricultural value of the land further south and its distance from the canal preserved it from the depredations of the brickmakers but not entirely from gravel extraction.

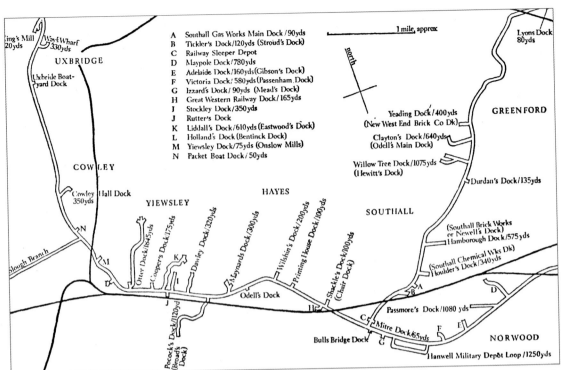

A   Southall Gas Works Main Dock / 90 yds
B   Tickler's Dock / 120 yds (Stroud's Dock)
C   Railway Sleeper Depot
D   Maypole Dock / 780 yds
E   Adelaide Dock / 160 yds (Gibson's Dock)
F   Victoria Dock / 580 yds (Passenham Dock)
G   Izzard's Dock / 90 yds (Mead's Dock)
H   Great Western Railway Dock / 165 yds
I   Stockley Dock / 350 yds
J   Rutter's Dock
K   Liddall's Dock / 610 yds (Eastwood's Dock)
L   Holland's Dock (Bentinck Dock)
M   Yiewsley Dock / 75 yds (Onslow Mills)
N   Packet Boat Dock / 50 yds

Map showing the docks leading from the canal. These docks, with few exceptions, were cut to provide access into the brickfields between Yiewsley and Hayes and at Yeading. This meant that barges could be readily loaded with bricks and taken by water to central London. On their return journey they could be loaded with London's rubbish for disposal in the worked-out pits. Nearly all the docks were on the north side of the canal and the area to the south remained largely free of the brickworks. (*Map reproduced from The Grand Junction Canal by A.H. Faulkner, David & Charles, 1972*)

Wooden Row, Stockley, just before demolition in 1935. These hovels were nicknamed 'Rabbit Hutch Row' and were built for the workers in the Stockley brickfields. They give a good insight to the extreme poverty of the conditions in which they lived. Similar conditions existed in the other brickfields and led a late nineteenth-century writer to remark of Yeading, 'sure I am that dirt, drunkenness and ignorance reign supreme' and that Botwell was little better. She added that 'the brick making may have something to do with the matter, for it seems one of the employments more especially carried on by profane workmen'.

Workers in the Starveall brickfields, *c.* 1897. James Crockett, third from left in the back row, with son Fred sitting next to him, daughter Nancy, 10 years old, in the straw boater, an unidentified fellow worker (standing, centre) and, in the front, his sons Arthur and James junior. Nancy is quite well dressed but the boys are bare-footed and the photograph is a good illustration of the wretched life of the workers in the brickfields. *(A. Beasley)*

Barges laden with rubbish from London arriving at Stockley, 1929. Domestic rubbish was brought by canal from central London to be dumped in the worked-out brickfields around Stockley and Yeading. The dumping was uncontrolled so that the land was rendered completely useless for any further development. The tips frequently caught fire, attracted vermin and were the source of many complaints. In 1929 Hayes Council complained to the Prime Minister that 'The Council regrets that the Minister of Health continues to neglect his duties in so much that he considers that the big Boroughs of London should be protected from the expense of dealing with their refuse in a sanitary manner to the detriment of the Urban and Rural areas'. Tipping at Yeading did not stop until 1948, however, and it continued for even longer at Stockley. Until 1912 Stockley was known as Starveall which, although the name long pre-dated the brickfields, was very apt once they had arrived. To improve its image it was renamed to give an association with the making of stock bricks. (WDLHS)

YIEWSLEY DUMP TROUBLE

Contractor to Pay £75 for Breaking Conditions

LARGE AREA LEFT UNCOVERED

MESSRS. H. SABEY & CO. were fined £60 and ordered to pay 15 guineas costs when they were summoned at Uxbridge Police Court on Monday for failing to comply with the conditions imposed by the Ministry of Health whereby they were allowed to continue dumping Wembley's refuse at Yiewsley.

The conditions not carried out were one requiring not less than 100 square yards of refuse to be uncovered at one time, and one requiring all faces of the refuse to be covered by nine inches of suitable material.

It was stated that on five days in July these conditions were not carried out, and that on one of the days there were 2,006 square yards of refuse uncovered.

Excerpt from the *Middlesex Advertiser and Gazette*, 5 September 1936. The dumping of London's rubbish in the worked-out brickfields at Stockley and Yeading was a continuing problem for the local authorities. The Middlesex County Council Act of 1934 laid down that the consent of the County Council and the local authority was needed if outside dumping was to be carried on. However, their powers were severely limited because the refuse disposal companies had the right of appeal against the authorities and frequently succeeded in gaining permission to dump. This meant that the authorities were restricted to ensuring that the dumping companies complied with the conditions imposed by central government. As can be seen from this newspaper cutting the conditions were not stringent but even so they were frequently ignored, leading to the problems seen in the next photographs. (The local paper was probably in error here, and the 'not less than 100 square yards' should surely have read 'not more than 100 square yards'.)

Unloading rubbish from barges, Horton Road, Yiewsley, 1929. *(WDLHS)*

Refuse dump behind Lawn Cottages, Stockley, 1929. The photograph taken from the canal towpath shows the indiscriminate nature of the dumping and the proximity of the dumps to houses.

Flies on the kitchen ceiling of 5 Lawn Cottages, 1929. The household refuse at the time contained a large amount of putrescible materials that attracted vermin and were a breeding ground for flies. The photograph shows the extent of the fly problem in the summer but rats must have been present in large numbers and the smell from the dumps appalling. Such conditions would not be tolerated today, but airlines regularly dump their noise and air pollution on the houses around airports in a manner that future generations may come to regard with horror. *(WDLHS)*

A scene in Stockley Road, 1977. The entrance to the works of a gravel-digging and refuse disposal company (H. Sabey), showing the generally run-down nature of the area until the renovations brought about by the Stockley Park development.

Stockley from the air, *c.* 1980, showing the utter devastation caused by the brickmaking and gravel industries and the subsequent uncontrolled backfilling. The view is to the north-west with the premises in the previous photograph seen towards the top left-hand corner with Stockley Road running past. What appears to be a road across the middle is an unsurfaced track.

Artist's impression of the Stockley Park development. Two-thirds of the 350 acres of derelict wasteland seen in the upper photograph were converted, in a programme of work beginning in the mid-1980s, into a country park and an 18-hole golf course. At the same time the former Stockley Road was partially re-aligned and upgraded to provide a bypass for Yiewsley and good access to the business park. To pay for these developments the southern part was converted into a business park. (*Stanhope plc*)

Stockley Park in 2003, looking south. Extensive landscaping and tree planting have converted the area south of Falling Lane and mostly (but not entirely) to the west of the Yiewsley bypass (Stockley Road) into a pleasant country park.

Stockley Business Park, 2003. Ready access to the canal and railway attracted manufacturing industry to the area in the early part of the twentieth century. A hundred years later the presence of Heathrow Airport and the motorway network has attracted a different type of industry. This is epitomised by the Stockley Park and London Gate developments (described later) which both provide excellent access to the M4, M25 and Heathrow Airport.

Another view of Stockley Business Park. The southern part of the Stockley area has been converted into a business park with low-rise office buildings among newly created lakes and a contoured landscape, which with the addition of extensive tree-planting has transformed the area into something far removed from that shown in the photographs of Stockley at the beginning of this chapter.

Less than 3 miles to the south-west of Stockley Park is Harmondsworth Moor, a large expanse of open land traversed by the many branches of the River Colne. It was, until the late 1950s, a very attractive area mostly in the ownership of Hillingdon Council and its predecessors. The councils leased the land for gravel extraction and, as owners of the land and as the local planning authorities, they were uniquely placed to impose any conditions that they wished for its eventual restoration. Sadly this was not the case and after the gravel had been extracted the holes were backfilled with rubbish so that the area became completely derelict, little better than the Stockley area before its rehabilitation.

Old gravel pit, Harmondsworth Moor, 1982. The pit was re-opened to provide material for the construction of the M25.

Harmondsworth Moor, 2000. In 1992 British Airways received planning permission to build its HQ offices on part of Harmondsworth Moor in return for agreeing to purchase the remainder of the Moor and rehabilitating it into a country park. The photograph shows BA's offices in the background and part of the Moor; this has been re-contoured and been extensively planted with trees to provide a park comparable with that at Stockley. However, BA is an improbable public benefactor and all is not as it may seem; for further discussion of this see Chapter 4, pp. 65ff.

Gravel digging, Little Harlington Field, Sipson Lane, 1991. Hillingdon Council regards the south of the borough as a source of income rather than as one of expenditure and, as the owners of the sports field, it gave permission for gravel to be extracted from this public playing field. Restoration conditions were written into the planning consent that required that it should eventually be restored within a stipulated time scale. This duly happened (see below) but it meant that for several years the various clubs that had used the field had to seek alternative sites outside the locality.

6

The Growth & Decline of Manufacturing Industry

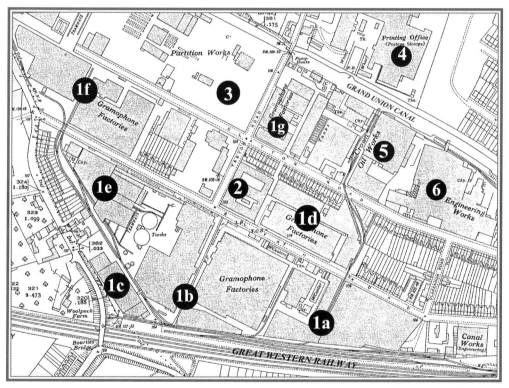

A 1935 Ordnance Survey map showing the position of the major factories. A former brickfield site in the Botwell area of Hayes bounded by the canal, the railway, Dawley Road and Station Road was acquired by the Hayes Development Company in 1900, and in the next few years the area came to be occupied by many factories. Some of the firms moving to the site were only short-lived; by 1935 the Gramophone Company (EMI) had taken over their premises and, as the map shows, had come to dominate the area.

1a–1g.	Factory buildings belonging to EMI (Gramophone Company)
2.	EMI Head Office
3.	Partition Works
4.	Harrison's Printing Works
5.	C.C. Wakefield Ltd (Castrol)
6.	British Electric Transformers

THE DEVELOPMENT OF HAYES.
ANOTHER LARGE NEW FACTORY.
PROMISING OUTLOOK FOR THE DISTRICT

The interesting little ceremony at Hayes last Saturday, when Mr Edward Lloyd the famous tenor cut the first sod in connection with the erection of the new works of the Gramophone and Typewriter Co. Ltd was a reminder of the fact that the industrial outlook at Hayes has become exceedingly bright of late years, thanks largely to the enterprise of the Hayes Development Co. and we have, consequently, secured full particulars concerning the various industries which have started at Hayes during the past few years.

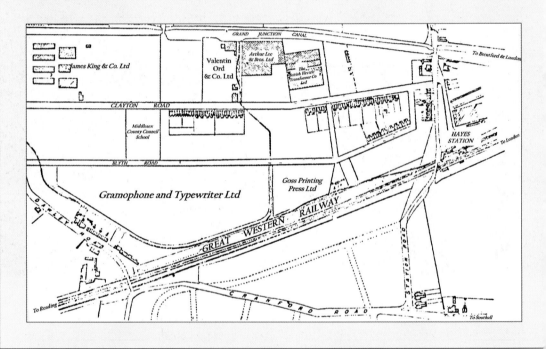

An article in the *Middlesex and Buckinghamshire Advertiser*, 16 February 1907, describing the progress of the Hayes Development Company Estate. The Gramophone Company was by far the most significant of the companies to move to the site but it was not the first. It was preceded by J.A. King & Co. in 1900 ('Mack' fireproof partitions), British Electric Transformers in 1901, Arthur Lee & Bros, in 1904 (marble, granite and slate), Goss Printing Press in 1905 and Valentine Ord & Co. in 1906 (saccharine, glucose, etc.).

The Gramophone Company (later EMI) was founded in 1897 when it acquired the UK rights to produce and market the gramophones and disc recordings that had been invented in the USA by Emile Berliner. In its early years it was based in London but in 1907 it moved to a site in between the railway line and Blyth Road, Hayes. The photograph shows building work in progress; typewriters had been made by the company for a short time as a hedge against the failure of the gramophone, but this fear proved to be unfounded and the company soon reverted to its original name. *(HHLHS)*

The photograph above shows the first factory buildings soon after completion. In 1899 the company had commissioned the artist Francis Barraud to modify his painting of a dog listening to a phonograph playing a cylindrical record of 'His Master's Voice'. The modification showed the dog listening instead to a disc recording playing on one of the company's gramophones. This became the registered trade mark of the Gramophone Company and achieved such fame that the company became better known by its trademark and the initials HMV. As can be seen in the lower photograph, most of the buildings in the photograph survive (2003). It is proposed that the middle building with its accompanying water tower should be adapted to become the Gate House of the London Gate development (see later). *(Above: K. Pearce)*

This building in Blyth Road is just to the east of the buildings shown in the previous photographs and like them was one of the early buildings on the site of the Hayes Development Company. At the time this photograph was taken in the late 1960s it had become part of the EMI complex and was occupied by EMI Records. It had, however, started life as the factory of the Goss Printing Press Company, which was occupied in the First World War as the National Aero Engine Company. It was then taken over by the McCurd Lorry Manufacturing Company in 1921 and between the windows at the top the letters 'URD LOR' can be seen painted on the brickwork. McCurds went into liquidation in 1927 and the building was taken over by the Gramophone Company. It was still standing in 2003 but was scheduled for demolition as part of the London Gate development. *(HHLHS)*

The former Head Office building of the Gramophone Company in Blyth Road, 2003. The company moved its head offices from London to Hayes in 1912. The building also contained the recording studios of the company until they were transferred to Abbey Road in 1931. With the removal of EMI from Hayes the building was converted to hostel accommodation and is now known as Jupiter House.

Enterprise House, Blyth Road, 2004. This was the first and arguably the ugliest of the multi-storey factory buildings to be erected for the Gramophone Company. It dates from 1912 and despite its brutal, no-nonsense functional appearance it alone among the buildings of the EMI complex is Grade II listed. This is because it is the first known work of Sir Owen Williams, the engineer-cum-architect, and is an early example of a reinforced concrete building. Its height and the water tank on top make it a distinctive feature which appears in the background to many of the photographs in this book. It acquired its current name when it was vacated by EMI and split up into warehousing and industrial units.

A publicity postcard from the early 1920s showing the original low-rise factory buildings in the middle. Behind them is the first multi-storey factory building to be constructed, to the left can be seen the Head Office of the company (see above). The two large factory buildings that now dominate the scene by the railway line and Bourne's Bridge (see p, 97) had not as yet been built. (HHLHS)

An aerial photograph of the factory complex from the 1930s. By then the Gramophone Company had merged (in 1931) with the Columbia Graphophone Company to become Electrical and Musical Industries (EMI), although for very many years after the merger the Gramophone Company and its HMV trademark were much better known to the general public. Comparison with the earlier illustration (above) shows that three large factory buildings had appeared in the intervening years. The expansion occurred because the company diversified its activities to include, in addition to its gramophone records, the manufacture, under the HMV name, of radios, radiograms, television sets and household appliances. (HHLHS)

The recording of an excerpt from Mendelssohn's 'Elijah', sung by boy soprano Ernest Lough in the early 1930s. It was the company's most successful recording from the 78rpm era, and sold 65,000 copies within six months of its release. Seventy years later it is still available on the HMV Classics label. The sleeve, which like the label was printed at Harrison's printing works, shows what was claimed to be the most advanced gramophone of the time and in the left-hand corner is an HMV portable gramophone that continued in production for the next twenty-five years.

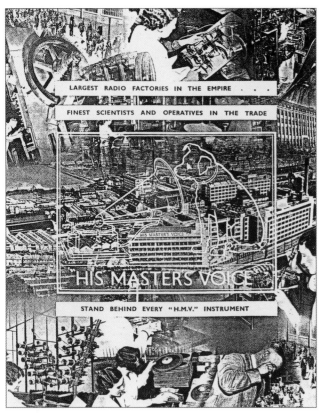

LARGEST RADIO FACTORIES IN THE EMPIRE . . .

FINEST SCIENTISTS AND OPERATIVES IN THE TRADE

HIS MASTERS VOICE

STAND BEHIND EVERY "H.M.V." INSTRUMENT

Company advertising from the 1930s. Although gramophone records still played an important part they became replaced in terms of the company's profits as it diversified into other fields. Much of the expansion was fuelled by the activities of the Central Research Laboratories. It was here that stereophonic recording and television in its present form was invented in the 1930s. Later inventions developed in the laboratories included the EMI body-scanner, for which EMI employee Godfrey Hounsfield was knighted and awarded the Nobel prize for physics. Ironically, the scanner, although an outstanding technical success, was to cause EMI severe problems when the company mishandled its marketing. Instead of licensing the use of its patents to other companies EMI tried to corner the large American market. This led the other companies to find ways of getting round the patents, and in a battle to protect them EMI lost a series of crippling court cases. As a result the company got into financial difficulties and was forced to merge (in what was virtually a takeover) with Thorn, a company with similar interests. The new company, known as Thorn-EMI, gradually closed its operations in Hayes until only the manufacture of records was left.

scipher

The EMI Group

EMI GROUP ARCHIVE TRUST

The introduction of compact discs led to the sudden collapse of the market for vinyl long-playing records and all that now remains of EMI activities in Hayes are the company archives in Dawley Road. In the meantime Thorn and EMI have de-merged and the wheel has turned full circle with the present-day EMI, like its ancestor the Gramophone Company, being solely concerned with the manufacture (but not in Hayes!) of recorded music. There were once 16,000 people employed by EMI in Hayes, but now no more than a handful remain to look after the company's valuable archives of recorded music covering a period of nearly 100 years.

Above: The HMV/EMI factory building on Bourne's Bridge, photographed during the early 1930s soon after the factory was built. *(Uxbridge Library) Below:* The same building in 2003, after refurbishment as office accommodation with its address as 'No. 1 London Gate' (see page 99). The open-plan nature of the floors of the factory building meant that it could easily be re-developed to provide floor-space that could be subdivided into offices. The photograph shows that all of the main features have been preserved and the building remains as a landmark on the bridge.

The old Bourne's Bridge was a dangerous bottleneck; it was completely rebuilt in the early 1990s to allow for the construction of the Heathrow–Paddington railway link but no attempt was made to straighten the road at the same time.

The new home of Rudge - Whitworth Limited .

THE new Rudge-Whitworth Factories, situate a few miles from the centre of London, have been planned in the light of seventy years rich experience. Here the Hand-built Rudge, with its numerous special features and outstanding quality, is produced in the Factory which represents all that is most modern and best in British Bicycle Manufacture.

RUDGE-WHITWORTH LIMITED
HAYES, MIDDLESEX

Further diversification of EMI occurred when in the late 1930s the company took over the Rudge Whitworth bicycle company of Coventry and moved its activities to a newly-built factory in Dawley Road. In the aerial view *(left)* of the Rudge Whitworth factory, the railway line and Bourne's bridge can be seen with the adjacent large EMI factory building just in the picture. The Rudge Whitworth building was to the west of Dawley Road and north of the railway line but, by the time this photograph was taken, EMI had sold the business (in 1944) to Raleigh Industries of Nottingham and was using the factory for the manufacture of tapes; it was later occupied by EMI Electronics. The factory was demolished in the late 1970s and the whole area has now been re-developed as an industrial estate known as Dawley Park. *(HHLHS)*

Aerial view of the Rudge Whitworth factory. *(HHLHS)*

The junction of Blyth Road with Dawley Road, *c.* 1960. At this time the EMI workforce numbered more than 16,000 so at the end of the day there was a huge exodus of work people disgorging on to the local roads. This photograph must have been taken just before or just after the main rush as a policeman is on point duty but relatively few people are present. In the early 1960s many people were still cycling to work. *(HHLHS)*

Artist's impression of Blyth Road as it will look after the refurbishment of the EMI factories into the London Gate development has been completed. The view is looking in the same direction as the upper photograph, and in both cases the large factory building (now known as Enterprise House and not part of the London Gate development) can be seen on the extreme left. *(London Gate PLC)*

Above and below: No. 2 London Gate from Blyth Road, 2003. The large factory complex of (Thorn) EMI gradually became redundant as the company closed down many of its activities and those that remained transferred to other parts of the country. For some years they remained empty but they are currently being refurbished as a development known as London Gate. The older single-storey buildings have mostly been demolished but most of the large factory buildings are gradually being converted to provide modern adaptable office accommodation. The site is close to Hayes station which already has a frequent service to Paddington with a 17-minute journey time, and will eventually have a direct link to Heathrow airport only 5 minutes away.

The British Electric Transformer Co. was one of the first companies to occupy the land acquired by the Hayes Development Company. It moved there in 1901 and in explaining the reason for making the choice it said, 'The question of transport, both for incoming and outgoing finished goods, received very careful attention before the Hayes site was finally decided on. As a result there are three methods of approach available, that is by road, rail or water.' The upper photograph shows the original works in Clayton Road and that on the right developments between 1901 and 1915. *(HHLHS)*

Aerial view of Botwell, *c.* 1932, with the BET factory in the centre. The canal runs diagonally across the lower half of the photograph and the railway line can just be seen in the left-hand corner. Between BET and the railway are the houses on the south side of Clayton Road and the north side of Blyth Road that were built at the same time as the factories to accommodate the workers. On the other side of canal to BET is Harrison's printing works (see page 110). *(HHLHS)*

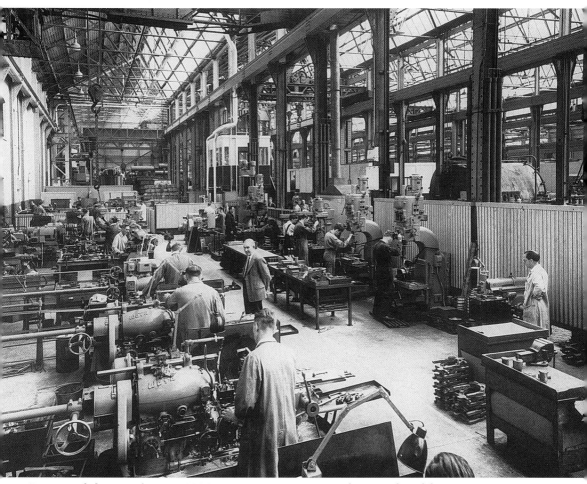

Interior of the BET factory, 1930s. Many contemporary photographs of factory interiors – EMI, Fairey Aviation (see page 107), Harrison Printing, etc. – look very similar, the only difference being the end product. Although transformers were the most important product, electrical equipment of all kinds such as electric kettles was also made by BET. Manufacturing industry of this type has completely disappeared from Hayes. This photograph together with the later interior photograph of the Fairey Aviation works well illustrates the sheer backbreaking drudgery of factory work at that time. Workers started work at 7.30 a.m. and were on their feet all day until 5 p.m. (12 noon on Saturday) with a short mid-morning break (which was then called lunch), a longer break at midday (then known as the dinner break) and another short break in the afternoon for a cup of tea. Factory sirens (hooters) summoned people to and from work; these were not synchronised so at times like 5 p.m. there was a cacophony of sirens blasting out from the various factories in Hayes. Although the profits of a company ultimately depended on the 'industrial' staff they were treated much worse than the office workers who were regarded as the real 'staff'. They had separate (and inferior) canteens and their terms of employment were such that they could be dismissed at short notice without pay at slack times and taken on again when work picked up. One of the worst offenders, which would have met with the approval of Ebenezer Scrooge, was the Gramophone Company which made its men work overtime to produce records for the Christmas trade and then laid many of them off just before Christmas. *(HHLHS)*

Level crossing, Station Road. The nucleus of the BET plant was built on the banks of the canal and GWR lines ran directly from Hayes station into the main workshops of the factory. To do this the trains had to cross Station Road and the photograph shows the level crossing that was just by the canal bridge. On the left of the picture is the Railway Arms, later demolished and replaced by The Tumbler and a tower block of offices. The Tumbler was demolished in 2003 and the office block converted to residential accommodation. *(J. Hayles)*

Opposite, above: Although at first most of the produce from the BET factory was sent by rail, by the 1930s the heaviest loads were being sent by lorry. Large overseas consignments were routed to Brentford by road and thence by Thames barge to the London Docks. The photograph shows a transformer on a low-loader leaving the Clayton Road factory. BET was taken over by Crompton Parkinson and this is the name that can be seen on the side of the trailer. Crompton Parkinson were in turn taken over by the Hawker-Siddeley Group and the Hayes factory was closed down in 1969. The large mast in the background belonged to the EMI Central Research Laboratories. *(HHLHS)*

Opposite, below: The factory of C.C. Wakefield Ltd in Clayton Road. The company was founded by Charles 'Cheers' Wakefield and specialised in selling industrial lubricants. Early in the twentieth century it moved to Hayes and began to produce motor oil, followed soon after by oils for motorcycles, aeroplanes and racing engines. In 1909 it launched the 'Castrol' brand name and the company was later renamed as 'The Castrol Group'. It was taken over by the Burmah Oil Company (now part of BP) in 1966 and the Hayes premises were closed. The factory had good access to the canal and a direct link to the railway line.*(HHLHS)*

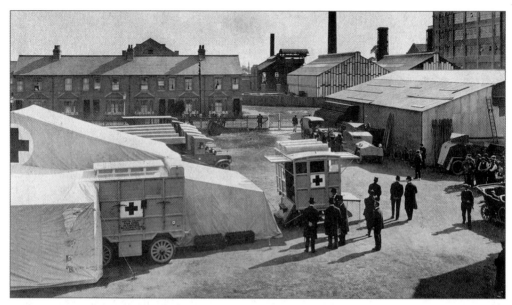

The premises in Clayton Road of the Army Motor Lorry and Waggon Co. This company was formed in 1915 to build transport vehicles for the Belgian army after most of Belgium had been occupied by the Germans. The photograph shows the factory yard in May 1915 occupied by a mobile field hospital with operating theatre and tented extensions. *(HHLHS)*

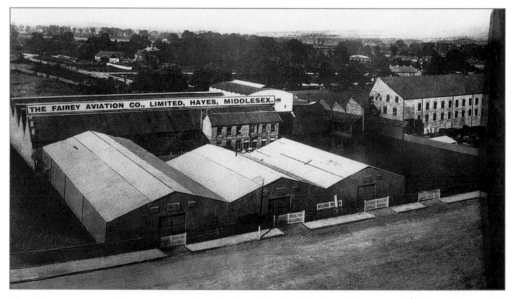

The Fairey Aviation Company was founded by (Charles) Richard Fairey in 1915 and began life in premises leased from the Army Motor Lorry and Waggon Co. in Clayton Road, Hayes. This photograph, dating from about 1916, shows the factory in Clayton Road but the name over the roof may be a photographic forgery because the factory did not belong to Fairey and similar photographs exist showing the name of the Army Motor Lorry Company, the actual owners of the factory, displayed prominently on the roof. Disputes between the companies led Fairey to do a moonlight flit; overnight he removed all of his equipment from Clayton Road to a site that he had acquired in North Hyde Road, Harlington. This site was subsequently developed as the headquarters and factory of the company. Because the company started life there the Hayes address was maintained although strictly speaking it was in Harlington.

Interior of the North Hyde Road works, *c.* 1917.

One of the First World War fighters produced by Fairey. It is standing in a field in North Hyde Road next to the company's factory. This ungainly beast, based on an Admiralty specification, would have had little chance against the more agile German fighters of the time. The view is to the north with the hedgerow of the road in the background and the ghostly silhouette of the Gramophone Company's multi-storey factory (now Enterprise House) in Clayton Road. Fairey's flight trials initially took place from this field but as the factory expanded it became too small for use. Later it obtained permission to use the RAF aerodrome at Northolt for its trials. When this permission was revoked it developed its own aerodrome at Heathrow in 1929 only to see this requisitioned by the Air Ministry in 1944 (see Chapter 4), thus beginning the slow decline of the company.

The company's factory in North Hyde Road, *c.* 1930. *(HHLHS)*

Aerial view of the factory, *c.* 1950, after it had expanded to its fullest extent so as to occupy most of the land bordered by Redmead Road, Station Road, North Hyde Road and Dawley Road. The loss of its aerodrome at Heathrow was a severe blow to the company particularly as it did not receive compensation for this loss until twenty years after it had been requisitioned! By then it had been taken over (in 1960) by Westland Helicopters, which closed the Hayes site in 1972 and moved its operations to Yeovil. *(HHLHS)*

The main office building of the Fairey Aviation Co., North Hyde Road. This was built in the 1930s and is the only building of the company that still stands on the site. It is now known as Mercury House and is used as offices by Safeway, the supermarket chain, who (in 2003) have warehouses occupying about one-third of the north-west corner of the Fairey site.

After the Fairey works were closed down by Westland in 1972 the site was re-developed as an industrial estate, consisting mostly of warehouses. By 2000 very few of the original firms remained and the office block that in this 1974 photograph was still under construction was demolished, together with most of the other warehouses apart from those belonging to Safeway on the northern half of the site. Three years later in 2003 the site was still vacant despite an advertisement hoarding claiming that it was a rare species ripe for development. (*J. Marshall*)

Harrison and Sons Ltd, Printing House Lane. This old family firm of printers acquired a site on the north side of the canal in 1911 and gave its name to the road that ran past the factory. It was outside but close to the sites of the factories that arrived as part of the Hayes Development Company's project. Harrison's main activities initially were the printing of stamps for the Post Office and printing for other government departments. After the GPO contract was lost in 1923 the firm diversified into other fields of printing, including record labels and sleeves for the nearby Gramophone Company. Harrison's moved from Hayes in the 1970s, and the factory was later demolished, but the name of Printing House Lane serves as a reminder of its existence. The upper photograph, from 1916, is an extended aerial view of the photograph that also appears on page 106. Harrison's factory is in the left-hand corner and to its left is the Blue Anchor public house. The lower photograph, from the same period, shows the factory, Printing House Lane and the Blue Anchor (the only building in the photograph that still remains). *(HHLHS)*

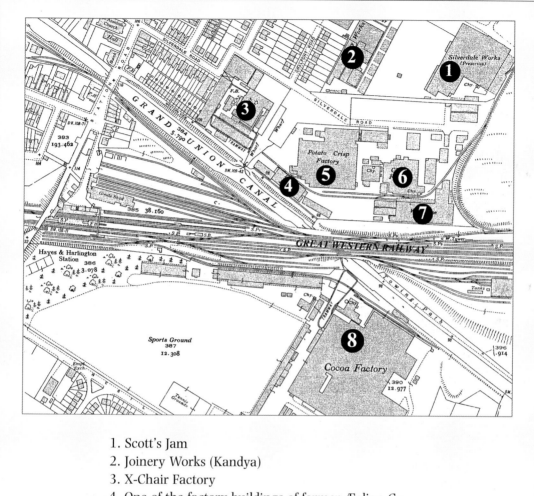

1. Scott's Jam
2. Joinery Works (Kandya)
3. X-Chair Factory
4. One of the factory buildings of former Æolian Co.
5. Potato Crisp Factory
6. Kraft Cheese
7. Factory building of former Vocalion Gramophone Co.
8. Nestlé (formerly Hayes Cocoa Co.)

An Ordnance Survey map of 1935, showing the major factories in the Silverdale Road area of Hayes. In addition to the factories on the Hayes Development Company's estate there was an almost equally intensive development in the area of Silverdale Road, which, as this map shows, originally had direct access to Station Road and was well placed to send and receive goods from the canal and the railway.

The X-Chair factory in Silverdale Road. This was one of the first factories to arrive in the area of Silverdale Road. It was founded in 1897 and opened its factory in Hayes in 1907. It closed down in 1948 but the factory buildings seen in this picture still remain and forms part of the Silverdale Road industrial estate. To the left of the X-Chair factory is the original building of the Æolian Company (see page 114). *(HHLHS)*

The X-Chair Company's exhibition stand at the British Industries Fair, 1934. *(HHLHS)*

MILESTONES 1897 · 1947

1897

Founded in the year of the Diamond Jubilee by the late Mr. A. E. Anderson, to whom we all owe a great debt of gratitude and who will be remembered by all who knew him with great admiration and respect. He was joined by Mr. A. W. Maxwell, who remained Chairman of the Company until his death in 1938 and by Mr. L. Pearson—father of our present Director—also on the Board. Business premises were acquired in Berry Street, Clerkenwell, and on the 5th August, 1897, we became incorporated as a Limited Company.

1901

In the year of the accession of King Edward VII to the throne it became necessary to move into larger premises at Provost Street, City Road.

1907

The Company was growing rapidly by this time and with an eye to future expansion, land was purchased at Hayes, Middlesex, a tiny village with only a shop or two and a sprinkling of cottages, surrounded by orchards and pastures. Silverdale Road was a rutted country lane and some of our older employees may remember seeing from the factory gate, the passing of the local Hunt, resplendent in scarlet, with the hounds in full cry.

1909

The first portion of the new building completed, we moved into the Hayes factory. Naturally, since those early days many changes have taken place ; more land has been purchased ; many additions and improvements have been made. More recently still a certain amount of demolition work was carried out by a notorious paperhanger with the peculiar name of Adolph Shicklegruber—but that is another story.

1914 - 1918

Hayes was growing rapidly and a number of other companies had erected factories in the vicinity. Then came the First World War and a large number of our men volunteered to serve their King and Country. Thus, with a depleted staff, we were called upon to make almost superhuman efforts to cope with the increasing demand for Camp Equipment by our Forces. For a period the factory was working 24 hours a day for seven days a week.

1919 - 1939

The period between the two Great Wars was possibly the most spasmodic in the history of the Company. After the immediate post war boom, came the worst slump in living memory. Nevertheless we managed to hold our own and from that time until 1939 business improved rapidly year by year. Then once again the Country was embroiled in a World War.

1940

On the 1st July this year our Company received the highest honour that can be bestowed upon an industrial concern by a reigning monarch when The " X " Chair Patents Company, Limited, was appointed suppliers of House and Garden Furniture by His Gracious Majesty, King George VI, and the Royal Warrant of appointment was granted to Mr. Wells, our Managing Director. Another recognition from a Foreign Power came in November, 1940, when we were visited by the Luftewaffe and three large bombs were dropped in the middle of our factory. Despite this, with the splendid co-operation of neighbouring companies and the loyal support of our own employees, production was resumed within a few days. Never once were we behind schedule with our Government contracts. A remarkable achievement !

1947

In reviewing the past fifty years we can, justifiably, be proud of our record, but now let us turn round and face the future with hope, courage and determination. It is extremely doubtful if many of us will be alive to look back upon the next fifty years, yet it must be remembered that it was largely due to those employees who did the spade work in the past, that we hold the position we do today. Let us, therefore, in the same spirit, forget silly prejudices and co-operate in making our own contribution to the general effort, so that in 1997 someone may be able to look back with equal pride on the results of the next fifty years.

The Company has served under five Monarchs and has been engaged on Work of National Importance during three Major Wars.

A brochure celebrating fifty years of the X-Chair Company, 1947. To celebrate the anniversary the whole workforce was taken to Windsor Castle followed by a steamer trip up the Thames. Reviewing the past fifty years, the company said it was justifiably proud of its record and would face the next fifty years with hope, courage and determination. But this was not to be: shortly afterwards a meeting of the directors took the decision to cease trading. (*J. Marshall*)

The Æolian, Weber Piano and Pianola Company of Massachusetts traded in Great Britain under many names including the Æolian Company, the Orchestrelle Company and the Weber Piano Company. In 1909 it opened a factory in Silverdale Road, seen here from the railway line shortly after it was opened. The main products of the company were mechanical piano players, a popular form of home entertainment before the days of recorded music and the radio. In 1912 the company became semi-independent of its American parent, with a registered office at the Æolian Hall in New Bond Street and a factory in Hayes. The central tower of the building was not just an architectural embellishment but was used for hanging the music rolls at full length during the manufacturing process. The photograph below (2003) shows that the original building still survives, surprisingly, although in a derelict state. It is in fact a fine red-brick building (Grade II listed) and well worthy of preservation as an example of early twentieth-century industrial architecture in Hayes. *(Above: HHLHS)*

Right: One of the products of the
Æolian/Orchestrelle Company.

CASEWORK OF HANDSOME DESIGN IS A FEATURE
---------------------- OF THE -----------------------

Pianola Piano

WE found that there was such a demand for special cases from purchasers of Pianola Pianos that we now always have in stock a certain number of models in cases of various special designs and woods. You would find these of the greatest interest, and we should be glad to show them whenever you care to call at Æolian Hall.

But of greater interest by far would be the Pianola Piano itself. You have only to get a Pianola Piano to be able to play all the music there is, and to realize to the full the immense fascination of personally producing music. Singled out by all the most famous musicians for its musical qualities and unique advantages such as the Metrostyle and Themodist, the Pianola Piano represents the finest piano investment offered today.

..................*Write for our catalogue AA which gives full particulars*..............

The Orchestrelle Co.

ÆOLIAN HALL
135–6–7 NEW BOND STREET, LONDON, W

Above: The Æolian Company had started to manufacture gramophone records under the Vocalion label from 1916 and later formed the Vocalion Gramophone Company in a factory adjoining its premises in Silverdale Road. From 1922 the company also produced cheaper records under the ACO label mostly for lighter music but this was replaced in 1927 by the Broadcast label. Broadcast records claimed to be long-playing, which was true in that an 8in record (as above) played for as long as a normal 10in record and a Broadcast 10in record could play as long as a normal 12in record. This was achieved by using a smaller label but only at the expense of the sound quality which deteriorated towards the end of the record.

A six-storey factory was built by the Æolian Company next to its original building in 1922 and, like the building seen in the background, it had a tower for hanging the music rolls at full length during the manufacturing process. One year later a factory for the newly formed subsidiary Vocalion Gramophone Company was built just to the right. *(HHLHS)*

The Æolian factory complex as seen from the railway line, *c.* 1960. The Æolian Company went into liquidation in 1932, and production of the company's gramophone records was taken over by the Crystalate Company (although not in Hayes and only until 1934). The Kraft McLaren Cheese Company took over the main factory building seen on the left. The Vocalion record factory in the right foreground was taken over by EMI and used mainly for storage. When Kraft Cheese left Hayes its factory building was acquired by Walls' Sausages, whose name appears on the tower. All the buildings in this photograph except the original factory of 1909 were demolished in the late 1970s. *(HHLHS)*

MESSRS. SANDOW'S
COCOA AND CHOCOLATE CO., LTD.

T HE Factory at Hayes, Middlesex, 11 miles from Paddington, was completed in 1914. It was designed by Messrs. Hal Williams & Company, London, the well-known Factory Architects and Specialists, and was built by Messrs. John Mowlem & Co., the well-known builders. It is absolutely modern and up-to-date in every respect, and stands on a site of some 38½ acres, which is acknowledged to be one of the best available near London. The Grand Junction Canal, by which direct access is obtained to the Port of London on the one hand, and to the Midland Towns and Coal Fields on the other, forms one boundary of the property. The Great Western Main Line, with every facility for any private sidings that may be required, forms another.

The Hayes Station is in immediate proximity, so that workpeople travelling by train have the minimum distance to walk to get to and from the Factory. The Railway Line is sufficiently high above the Site to make the advertising advantages of the site of exceptional value. The Great Western Railway Company have scheduled a strip of land about 100 feet wide alongside their line for compulsory purchase for the purpose of widening their line, and the vacant portion of the site has been commandeered by the Government for military purposes for the period of the war. In this connection a Railway Siding has been put in, and will in all probability be available for ordinary goods traffic when the Government relinquish the property.

An Extensive business in the manufacture and sale of Cocoa and the sale of Chocolate is being and has been carried on by the Vendors at the Factory since the completion of its erection in 1914, and particulars of the Turnover of the Company will he supplied to bona fide Purchasers upon application in writing to the Company's Manager at Hayes.

The essential particulars of the Factory and Site are summarised as follows:

Sandow's Cocoa Factory, Hayes, Middlesex

Sale details of Sandow's Cocoa and Chocolate Company, *c.* 1918. The company was founded by the amazing Eugene Sandow, the legendary strongman of the music hall. He could lift a grand piano over his head, and once fought a lion and won! After retiring from the stage he opened several physical culture centres. He convinced himself of the value of cocoa as a health food and so decided to sell it commercially. A 42-acre site was acquired just south of the canal and the factory was completed by 1914. He ran into financial difficulties and in 1919 the factory was taken over by a Swiss-owned company known as the Hayes Cocoa Company. This in turn was taken over by Nestlé in 1929 and the factory which has been very much extended still remains. Nestlé is also a Swiss company and the acute accent on the last 'e' clearly means that it should be pronounced as 'Nestlay'. However, to do so locally would be considered to be an affectation and it is always pronounced as spelt without the accent. (*Uxbridge Library*)

The Hayes Cocoa Company was taken over by Nestlé in 1929, which alone among the companies described in this chapter still retains a significant presence in Hayes. This photograph from the early 1930s shows the major additions made by Nestlé to the original Sandow factory, which can be seen as darker in colour to the new additions.

Scott's jam factory, Pump Lane, early 1930s. The factory occupied a position fronting on to Pump Lane and backing on to Silverdale Road. It was opened by Scott's in 1914 and closed in the 1950s. In 1960 the factory was acquired by Callard & Bowser, Nuttall Ltd, a subsidiary of Arthur Guinness, which gradually moved much of its production of confectionery to Hayes. By 1980 three-quarters of all the toffees made in the UK originated from the Hayes factory. However, the factory was closed by Guinness in the mid-1980s and the building was demolished. *(HHLHS)*

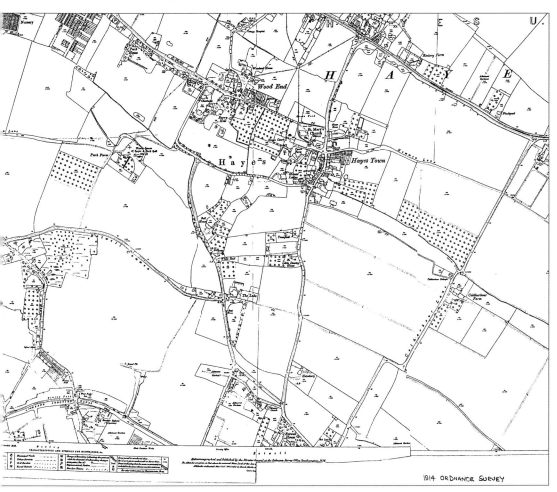

An Ordnance Survey map of Hayes in 1914. At the end of the nineteenth century the population of Hayes was only 2,500 and it was still a rural community. By 1931 it had become heavily industrialised and the population had increased almost tenfold to 25,000. This rapid expansion caused a severe housing shortage, and a survey by the local paper in 1911 revealed that two-thirds of the Hayes workforce were obliged to live elsewhere as house building could not keep pace with the industrial development that was occurring. The Hayes UDC did undertake housing projects in the district even before the First World War, and after the Housing & Town Planning Act of 1919 the problem of overall supply of low rent housing became a local authority responsibility. With subsidies granted under a separate Housing (Additional Powers) Act, a scheme was drawn up for the building of 2,000 houses. The acquiring of land for this scheme now became the principal focus of attention of the Hayes UDC. *(J. Walters)*

An Ordnance Survey map of Hayes in 1935. The council identified and designated a triangular area of land bounded by Church Road, Coldharbour Lane and the Uxbridge Road as having the potential to cope with the number of houses to be built. The two maps here and on page 119 show how this area had come to be completely infilled by houses by 1935. But even this was not enough and by 1929 the local paper estimated that 12,000 people travelled daily to work from outside the immediate area of their workplace because they could not find local accommodation. Still more houses came to be built so that the population had almost trebled between 1931 and 1951 to reach 66,000 (this figure also included Harlington as that part of Harlington close to the station had also been intensively developed for housing). The sudden concentration of industry and huge growth in population in such a relatively small area was a matter of some concern. It led the Greater London Development Plan of 1944 to remark that 'these intense concentrations of industry on the best agricultural land have created grave housing difficulties and should not be encouraged to grow'. (*J. Walters*)

7

The Limits to Growth

Sustainable Development – Development that meets the needs of the present without compromising the ability of future generations to meet their own needs. If our lifestyles are not sustainable they will have to be modified sooner or later.

Royal Commission on Environmental Pollution, 1994

Transport by road and air has grown at an ever increasing pace over the last 100 years and to meet this growth the Department for Transport has during this time adopted a policy known as 'Predict and Provide'. In essence this means that predictions are made of the anticipated growth in the particular form of transport, based on a study of past trends, and then provision of the transport infrastructure has been provided to meet this predicted growth. This policy has been criticised partly because it is to some extent self-fulfilling – the predicted growth becomes a target to be achieved and the traffic expands to fill the capacity provided.

However, a much more serious criticism is that in recent years it has become increasingly obvious that the predicted growth cannot go on forever because in the long term it is simply not sustainable. Thus in its report *Transport and the Environment* (1994) the Royal Commission on Environmental Pollution stated: 'An unquestioning attitude towards future growth in air travel and an acceptance that the projected demand for additional facilities and services must be met are incompatible with the aim of sustainable development.' This conclusion was made with respect to air travel but it is equally true of road transport.

The problem has arisen because of the change to mechanical form of propulsion based on the combustion of fossil fuels. Until the end of the eighteenth century all forms of land transport were based almost exclusively on horse-drawn vehicles. Air traffic did not exist and water-borne traffic depended principally on wind-power. Transport did not therefore involve any depletion of natural resources and was indefinitely sustainable.

However, from the early nineteenth century transport became increasingly dependent on mechanical power, based first on the burning of coal and then oil to produce the energy required. These are essentially hydrocarbons with, in the case of oil, the empirical formula $C_nH_{2n}+2$. For example, octane with eight carbon atoms is, C_8H_{18} and the combustion of this in air is represented by the equation:

$$2C_8H_{18} + 25O_2 = CO_2 + 18H_2O + \text{energy}$$
$$\text{octane} + \text{oxygen} = \text{carbon dioxide} + \text{water} + \text{energy}$$

From this equation it is easy to calculate that theoretically the combustion of 100g of octane will give rise to the production of 309g of carbon dioxide (CO_2). This is a basic fact of chemistry and there is absolutely no possibility of reducing the amount of carbon dioxide that is produced other than to reduce the amount of fuel that is burnt.

The equation assumes that combustion is 100 per cent efficient but in an internal combustion engine this is never the case, which means that carbon dioxide and water (H_2O) are not the only combustion products. Because the fuel is not completely oxidised the exhaust gases contain small proportions of unburned fuel and partially-

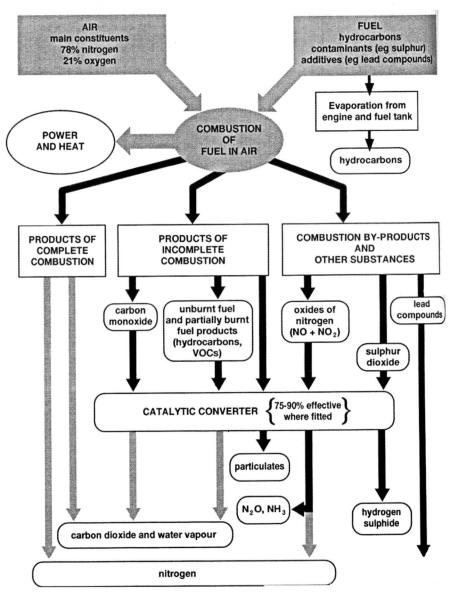

Combustion of hydrocarbons in an internal combustion engine. (Royal Commission on Environmental Pollution 2002)

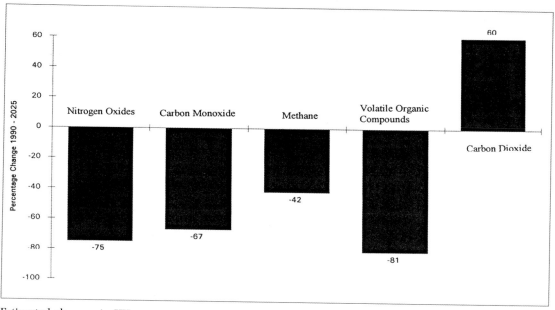

Estimated changes in UK passenger car gas emissions 1990–2025. *(K.D. Mason,* Road Transport and the Environment – The Future Agenda in the UK, *1993)*

burnt fuel products – hydrocarbons and volatile organic compounds (VOCs) – plus nitrogen oxides derived from the oxidation of the nitrogen in the air at the high temperatures prevailing inside the combustion chamber of the engine.

In contrast to the fuel, which is not particularly toxic, many of the partially burnt fuel products and the nitrogen oxides emitted are highly toxic even in small concentrations. However, the amount of these can be reduced – but not completely eliminated – by the fitting of catalytic converters. This is expected to make a significant reduction in the problem (see below) but improvements in engine technology are being over-taken by the growth in traffic so that the reduction may be less than predicted.

The previous figures might suggest that the problem of toxic emissions can be largely overcome but in the vicinity of large transport termini such as airports the growth and the intensity of the traffic cancels out any reduction in the emissions from an individual source. A good (or bad) example of this is provided by Heathrow Airport, as illustrated by the newspaper cutting on the next page that shows the extent of pollution from nitrogen oxides around the airport.

Because of these pollution problems the government had to concede in 2003 that it would fall foul of EU regulations if it granted permission for the construction of a third runway at Heathrow. It therefore postponed the decision until 2015 by which time it was hoped that improvements in aircraft engine technology would reduce the emissions of toxic pollutants. However, the Royal Commission on Environmental Pollution has pointed out that 'Despite the considerable opportunities for incremental improvements to the environmental performance of individual aircraft these will not offset the effects of growth'. (Royal Commission on Environmental Pollution, 2002)

DEATHROW AIRPORT

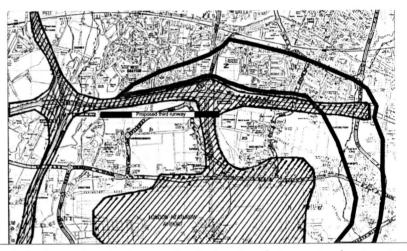

Front page of

"The Hayes Gazette"

25 September 2002

Map of air pollution around Heathrow airport. The cross-hatched section that occupies the airport itself and the areas immediately adjacent to the M4 and M25 shows the area which in 2002 already exceeded permitted levels of nitrogen oxide emissions laid down by EU regulations. Even if no third runway were to be built the anticipated increase in traffic by 2015 would take the area affected by harmful levels of NOx up to the boundaries of the M4 and M25. This would expose 10,000 people to illegal levels of pollution so they would have to leave their homes. With a third runway in place the boundary for toxic emissions would be extended into the area marked by the heavy black line to the north of the M4 and the east of the airport. This would take the number of people affected by harmful emissions of NOx up to 35,000.

The map shows that a good deal of the pollution around Heathrow derives from road traffic on the M4 and M25. To overcome this problem it has been seriously suggested that the M4 should be put into a 4-mile long tunnel between junctions 3 and 4b. The tunnel would need to be equipped with scrubbers to remove the nitrogen oxide emissions. The cost of constructing the tunnel would be such as to make it economical only if motorists were charged £20 to use it!

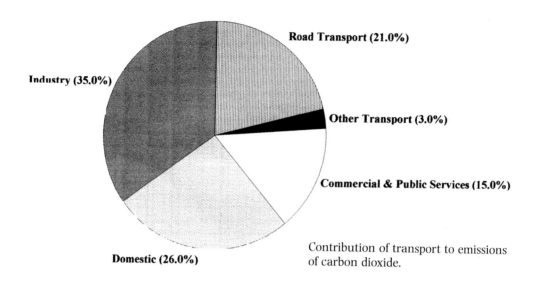

Contribution of transport to emissions of carbon dioxide.

If the combustion products of vehicles and aircraft were confined merely to the toxic gases mentioned previously the problem might be contained. However, the earlier figure also shows that it is estimated that the amount of carbon dioxide emitted by road vehicles is expected to increase by 60 per cent. As can be seen from this pie chart, in 1990 transport already accounted for one-quarter of all carbon dioxide emissions. More recent estimates show that as other sources of carbon dioxide are reduced in line with the government's commitment to reduce greenhouse gases the contribution from transport will increase to 50 per cent of the total by 2050.

Carbon dioxide is not toxic, it is a natural constituent of the air and without it life on earth could not exist. Until recently release of the gas into the atmosphere was not therefore considered to be a problem. The Earth naturally absorbs and reflects incoming solar radiation and emits longer wavelength terrestrial (thermal) radiation back into space. On average, the absorbed solar radiation is balanced by the outgoing terrestrial radiation emitted to space. A portion of this terrestrial radiation, though, is itself absorbed by gases such as carbon dioxide in the atmosphere. The energy from this absorbed terrestrial radiation warms the Earth's surface and atmosphere, creating what is known as the 'natural greenhouse effect'; so named because a similar phenomenon occurs inside a greenhouse where the temperature inside a greenhouse is much higher than it is outside.

As a result of the natural greenhouse effect the temperature of the atmosphere is significantly higher than it would otherwise be. This is beneficial and while the concentration of the greenhouse gases in the atmosphere remained at their historic levels the temperature of the atmosphere was unlikely to increase beyond the values to which all forms of life had become accustomed. However, the concentration of carbon dioxide in the atmosphere is rapidly rising as a result of the burning of fossil fuels. Before the industrial revolution the concentration of carbon dioxide in the atmosphere was 278 parts per million (ppm); by 1998 it had risen to 365ppm and it will rise still further if nothing is done to reduce manmade emissions of the gas. This means that the temperature of the atmosphere is gradually increasing giving rise to global warming.

This is a very serious problem with possible catastrophic consequences. This fact is recognised by the government which in early 2003 issued a White Paper on energy. The White Paper is supposed to commit the government to a 'low-carbon' economy in which carbon dioxide emissions would be cut by 60 per cent over the next 50 years. During the same week that the White Paper was published the Department for Transport saw fit to re-issue the airport consultation papers, predicting a threefold increase in air travel over a shorter period! If these predictions were realised the amount of carbon dioxide emitted by the aviation industry would at least double even allowing for improvements in fuel economy.

As discussed earlier it is a matter of simple chemistry that the combustion of aviation fuel will give rise to the production of carbon dioxide and for a given amount of fuel the carbon dioxide emissions can be accurately calculated. If the aviation industry and road transport is allowed to expand and the White Paper is to be taken seriously it will therefore inevitably mean that the other sources of carbon dioxide emission will have to reduce their contribution to carbon dioxide emissions not by 60 per cent but by a far larger amount! The immediate question is why should they?

Another factor to consider is that the supplies of fossil fuels are not infinite and oil is already being consumed at a faster rate than the discovery of new sources. Sooner rather than later transport will have to switch from oil to another source. Electricity is one possibility, provided that it is not generated by the burning of fossil fuels. Hydrogen has also been suggested as a fuel and it has the advantage that the only combustion product is water. But although in theory the supply is inexhaustible, it does not occur in elemental form and the most probable source would be by the electrolysis of water. This again requires the input of energy and the laws of thermodynamics means that at least as much energy would be used up in producing it as would be released from its combustion. This can be seen from the equations for the production (1) and combustion (2) of hydrogen, where the energy needed in equation (1) equals the energy produced in equation (2):

$$(1)\ 2H_2O + energy = 2H_2 + O_2$$
$$(2)\ 2H_2 + O_2 = 2H_2O + energy$$

The balance of energy in the equations assumes 100 per cent efficiency but, in practice, this is never the case. So the amount of energy required to produce hydrogen will always exceed the amount of energy produced from its combustion by a substantial amount.

Air pollution monitoring station, Sipson Lane, Harlington. This is one of several installed around Heathrow airport to measure the extent of air pollution arising from aircraft and road traffic. Because the concentration of nitrogen oxides in the immediate vicinity of the airport already exceeded the limits laid down by EU regulations, the government was unable to accede to the demands of the aviation industry for the construction of a third runway at Heathrow. The decision was postponed from 2003 to 2015 in the hope that by then the air pollution could be reduced to acceptable levels and the monitoring stations are part of the assessment programme. However, it is highly probable that the limits to growth at Heathrow have already been reached if not surpassed.

In the background about 1 mile away the village of Sipson can be seen; this would be destroyed if Heathrow were to be expanded. The open land in the photograph shows how easy it would subsequently be to extend a third runway further east to engulf Harlington.

INDEX